THE GIFT OF INFALLIBILITY

The Official Relatio on Infallibility
of Bishop Vincent Gasser
at Vatican Council I

Translated, with commentary
and a theological synthesis on infallibility,
by

Rev. James T. O'Connor

ST. PAUL EDITIONS

NIHIL OBSTAT:
   Francis J. McAree, S.T.D.
   Censor Deputatus
IMPRIMATUR:
   ✠ Joseph T. O'Keefe, D.D.
   Vicar-General, Archdiocese of New York

Library of Congress Cataloging-in-Publication Data

Gasser, Vinzenz, 1809-1879
    The gift of infallibility.

    1. Popes—Infallibility. 2. Catholic Church—Infallibility.
I. O'Connor, James Thomas. II. Title.

BX1806.G3413   1986   262'.131   86-2063

ISBN 0-8198-3042-9
     0-8198-3041-0 (pbk.)

Printed in the U.S.A., by the Daughters of St. Paul
50 St. Paul's Ave., Boston, MA 02130

The Daughters of St. Paul are an international congregation of women religious serving the Church with the communications media.

In Memory of
Pope Paul VI

CONTENTS

Introduction

The gift of infallibility, given by the Lord to His Church and to St. Peter and his successors as chief teachers and pastors of the Church, has, along with many other truths, become a matter of renewed theological discussion and contention since the close of the Second Vatican Council in 1965. The doctrine of infallibility, which holds that the Church and the Pope are, in specific and determined circumstances, not able to make a mistake when teaching matters of faith and morals which must be held by all the faithful, has itself been declared to be—insofar as the Pope is concerned—a matter of faith which has been divinely revealed. This definition of faith was proclaimed at the First Council of the Vatican (1869-1870) during the pontificate of Pope Pius IX (1846-1878).

Much has been written about the development of the doctrine of infallibility and about the meaning of chapter four of the Dogmatic Constitution *Pastor Aeternus* in which the bishops at Vatican I solemnly taught the infallibility of the Pope. Central to all the discussions on the meaning of papal infallibility as Vatican I defined it has been the official presentation, the relatio, made by Bishop Vincent Ferrer Gasser to the general congregation of bishops of Vatican I which took place on July 11, 1870.

Dom Cuthbert Butler, whose work *The Vatican Council* in two volumes,[1] although long out of print, remains the most complete history of the Council in English, wrote: "Msgr. Vincent Gasser, Prince-Bishop of Brixen, Austrian Tyrol, stands out as the most prominent theologian of the Council."[2] History has confirmed that judgment. So important is the relatio of Gasser that it has itself become a *theological source,* cited in innumerable manuals and theological treatments and serving even in our own times as a key element in the renewed theological discussions about infallibility. Indeed the Second Vatican Council, in its Dogmatic Constitution on the Church *(Lumen Gentium),* cites Gasser's relatio four times in its important chapter on the magisterium or teaching office of Pope and bishops. Paragraph #25 has approximately only 55 lines of text and eight official footnotes. Thus, half of the citations in that key section of Vatican II's *Lumen Gentium* are to Gasser's relatio.

Despite its importance in all theological discussion on the doctrine of infallibility, Gasser's relatio has never, as far as I can determine, been translated from the Latin original into English. Butler's work devotes a chapter to it, and translates or paraphrases about one third of the original,[3] thereby highlighting most of the key issues, but also omitting several significant points. The result is that a major theological source remains unavailable to all those who do not have the time, or proficiency in Latin to tackle the twenty-six long columns of the original as found in *Mansi.*[4]

Vincent Gasser was born in 1809, taught dogmatic theology after ordination to priesthood, was nominated by the Emperor Franz Joseph as prince-bishop of Brixen in the Tyrol in 1856 and died there as bishop in 1879. The importance of his role at Vatican Council I can be gathered from the following considerations.

In order to facilitate their work, the bishops at Vatican I established various commissions or deputations to act as what might be called "clearing centers" for the work of the Council. Probably the most important of these commissions was the Deputation *de fide* to which was ultimately entrusted the work of producing a draft document on papal infallibility. The members of the Deputation *de fide* were all elected by the bishops of the Council from a list drawn up by Archbishop Manning of Westminster, England, the leader of those favoring the definition of papal infallibility. The Deputation consisted of twenty-four members, among whom were Manning, Victor Dechamps of Belgium, Ignatius Senestrey of Ratisbon, John Spalding of Baltimore, U.S.A., the primates of Hungary and Poland (then part of the German Empire), Pie of Poitiers, France, and Gasser. Only the primate of Hungary, John Simor, belonged to that minority of bishops at the Council which did not favor a definition of papal infallibility.

After its initial meetings, the Deputation presented to the bishops a draft (hereafter referred to as the Draft) of chapter four for the Constitution *Pastor Aeternus*. That Draft, found on pages 9-10 following, was accepted by the bishops at the Council as their working document, to be changed or emended after discussion and voting. The Draft consisted of two long paragraphs. Two days before Gasser gave his relatio, however, the Deputation proposed certain changes in the Draft, changes which were to be inserted between paragraphs one and two of the Draft. The Deputation had also reworked the actual definition (paragraph two of the Draft), and all of Gasser's remarks in his relatio refer to the Draft and these changes. These changes and the proposed new form of the definition follow on pages 11-13. In addition to the changes proposed by the Deputation itself, long discussions in the general congregations of the bishops had resulted in over seventy other suggested changes in the Draft. The Deputation had the task of reviewing each of these suggestions and of recommending to the bishops what action should be taken on them.

The Deputation then entrusted to Gasser the task of relaying its recommendations, and of giving an *official explanation* of the meaning of the emended Draft so that the bishops would know precisely what they were voting on when they came to approve or reject the proposed chapter four of *Pastor Aeternus*. It is in this aspect of his task that the importance of Gasser's relatio can be discerned. It is the key to proper interpretation of chapter four of *Pastor Aeternus* as it was finally approved since the bishops voted on it as explained by Gasser representing the Deputation *de fide*.

As given by Gasser, the relatio of July 11 took almost four hours to deliver, and that despite the fact that his style is precise, clear and, with one exception, not given to digressions. The relatio reveals a mind which is logical in process and fully acquainted with the historical and theological aspects of the question at hand. The talk is devoid of polemical attacks against the minority which did not want a definition of papal infallibility, and gives no ground to those of the bishops who wanted what might be called an "extremist" view of papal infallibility to be defined. At first glance, the relatio given by Bishop Gasser seems to contain little that is new to us. It *appears* to be the standard understanding of what Vatican I defined vis-à-vis papal infallibility. A careful reading, however, will produce some "surprises," especially in regard to what is meant by the word "define" as it is used in the definition of papal infallibility and in regard to what matters are to be held as capable of being included in an infallible definition of the Pope.

Gasser delivered his relatio at a time when the whole ambit of discussion on infallibility was somewhat different from the one we experience after a second Vatican Council. Some aspects of recent discussion were outside his perspective; questions have been raised which he did not foresee, and could not have foreseen. I have had to resist the temptation to re-read Gasser's relatio in the light of recent controversies and of the various uses made of his relatio by theologians of opposing views. Therefore I have kept the commentary to the minimum I considered necessary to clarify what Gasser himself said, hoping thereby to offer his work as a source and not as one more partisan treatise in the ongoing discussions on infallibility.

What commentary there is will be found in smaller print at the foot of Gasser's text. The numerical references in the margins are to the *Mansi* columns of the original, and, to facilitate reference to the original, I have retained the same paragraph structure as is found in the original.

The Second Vatican Council, which in its own teaching on the Magisterium of the Church uses Gasser's relatio as a source, has, of course, set the question of papal infallibility in the context of the infallibility or indefectability of the entire

Church. In part for that very reason, I have written the final chapter which deals with the topic of infallibility in this wider perspective as the Church teaches it. In that chapter I have tried to present an overview of the entire question of infallibility with an effort to keep the question less "specialized" than is Gasser's relatio or the commentary on it. I have also tried to arrange it in such a way that it can be used as a type of "study guide" to the relatio of Bishop Gasser. In this way, hopefully, the work may be of value to the general student as well as to the specialist. Even there, however, I have generally avoided going into the recent specific controversies on infallibility, most of which, indeed, were not theological in the strict sense but involved, rather, the philosophical questions which touch upon the mind's ability to know the truth, to know it definitively, and to express it—in respect to revealed truth—at least adequately. Such questions, of course, merit a special treatment of their own but for our purpose we begin from the Church's own premise, viz., that God has given the human mind, either by its own natural powers or through the gift of faith, the ability to know reality—even revealed reality—as it truly is, and that this ability is never completely lost, even by sin.

A special word of thanks is due to Fr. Donald W. Hendricks of St. Anthony's Parish, Yonkers, New York, who generously reviewed the translation for errors. Any that might remain are due to my own negligence.

This little work is dedicated to the memory of that great and saintly man who guided the Church through the Second Vatican Council and the years which followed it. His witness to the truth—so often bitterly contested—was itself a gift to the Church.

Footnotes

1. Butler, *The Vatican Council,* Longmans, Green and Co., N.Y., 1930.
2. *Idem,* II, p. 134.
3. *Idem,* pp. 134-148.
4. *Collectio Conciliorum Recentiorum, Mansi,* vol. 52, 1927, Arnhem, Holland, 1204ff.

Texts Used by Gasser

First Draft
of Chapter IV
on Papal Infallibility

Chapter IV—
On the Infallibility of the Roman Pontiff

Moreover in the supreme power of apostolic jurisdic- [6] tion which the Roman Pontiff holds in the universal Church as successor of Peter, the Prince of the Apostles, there is included the supreme power of teaching. This Holy See has always held this [truth], the perpetual usage of the Church approves it, and the ecumenical councils themselves have taught it. Therefore, following especially the general councils in which the East and West came together in a union of faith and charity, we, together with Constantinople IV, believe the solemn profession of faith which says: "The first thing required for salvation is to preserve the rule of the true faith and to deviate in no way from what was decreed by the holy Fathers. And because it is not possible to set aside the words of Our Lord Jesus Christ when He says, 'You are Peter and on this rock I will build my Church,' we see that these words are proved true by events, because the Catholic faith has always been preserved immaculate in the Apostolic See, and its doctrine kept holy. Christ's faithful are held to follow this Apostolic See in all things so that they may deserve to be in

one communion with that same See in which there is present
[7]   the whole and true security of the Christian religion." And,
with the Second Council of Lyons, we profess: "The Holy
Roman Church holds the supreme and full primacy and
power over the universal Catholic Church. She humbly and
truly recognizes that she has received this, with the fullness of
power, from the Lord Himself in Blessed Peter, the Prince or
Head of the Apostles; and since, before all others, she is held
to defend the truth of the faith, if any questions should arise
concerning the faith, they should be defined by her [i.e., the
Roman Church's] judgment." And with the Council of Florence we repeat: "The Roman Pontiff stands as the true Vicar
of Christ, the head of the whole Church and the father and
teacher of all Christians; to him has been given, in Blessed
Peter, the full power of shepherding, ruling and governing
the universal Church."

Hence, with the approval of the sacred council, we teach
and declare that it is a dogma of faith that the Roman Pontiff, to whom, in the person of Blessed Peter, it has been said,
among other things, by the Lord Jesus Christ, "I have prayed
for you that your faith may not fail and, when you have
turned, strengthen your brothers," by the power of the divine
assistance promised to him, is not able to err when, exercising
his office as supreme teacher of all Christians, he defines, by
his apostolic authority, what must be held as belonging to the
faith or must be rejected as contrary to the faith by the universal Church in matters of faith and morals; and his decrees
or judgments, irreformable of themselves, must be accepted
and held with the full submission of faith as soon as one
becomes aware of them. Because this infallibility, whether
taken from the point of view of the Roman Pontiff as head of
the Church or from that of the universal Church teaching,
united with its head, is the same, we further define that this
infallibility also extends to one and the same object. If anyone
should presume to contradict this definition of ours (God
grant that this not happen), let him know that he has
departed from the truth of the Catholic faith and from the
unity of the Church.

Corrections Proposed by the Deputation
de fide *on July 9, 1870*

6. The Deputation *de fide* proposes that suggested cor- [1194]
rections #10, 73, 75, 76, 77, and 78, adopted by the general
congregation, be inserted in the following manner [into the
proposed chapter].

"To satisfy this pastoral office, our predecessors always
expended untiring effort to see that the saving doctrine of
Christ be propagated among all the peoples of the earth, and,
with equal care, they watched that it might be preserved pure
and sincere where it had been received. Therefore, the bishops of the whole world, sometimes individually, sometimes
gathered in synods, following the 'long-established custom of
the Churches' and 'the manner of the ancient rule [of faith]'
reported back to this Apostolic See those special dangers
which arose in matters of faith, so that harm to the faith
might be especially repaired in that place where the faith can
suffer no defect. Moreover, the Roman Pontiffs, according to
the dictates of time and circumstances, sometimes by calling
ecumenical councils or asking the opinion of the Church
dispersed throughout the world, sometimes through particular synods, sometimes by using other means which divine
providence supplied, defined those things which must be
held and which they knew, by the help of God, to be consonant with the Sacred Scriptures and apostolic traditions. For
the Holy Spirit promised to the successors of Peter, not that
they would unfold new doctrine which He revealed to them,
but that, with His assistance, they would piously guard and
faithfully expound the revelation or deposit of faith handed
on through the Apostles. All the venerable Fathers and holy
orthodox doctors venerated and followed their [i.e., the successors of Peter] apostolic doctrine; they knew full well that
this See of St. Peter always remained unstained by all error,
according to the divine promise which Our Savior made to
the chief of His disciples when He said, 'I have prayed for
you, that your faith may not fail, and you, having turned,

strengthen your brothers'; nor were they ignorant of the fact that it is necessary that every church, i.e., all the faithful everywhere, agree with the Roman Church, nor of the fact that the Roman Pontiffs were not able to reply to those seeking the truth of the faith except with what the ancient Apostolic See and Roman Church perseveringly holds, together with the other churches.

"Therefore this charism of truth and unfailing faith was divinely given to Peter and his successors in this chair so that they might fulfill their high office for the salvation of all, so that the whole flock of Christ might, through them, be turned away from the poisonous food of error and be fed on the food of heavenly doctrine, and so that, every occasion of schism being removed, the whole Church might be preserved as one and, firmly grounded on its foundation, might stand against the gates of hell.

"Since in our times, which especially require the salvific efficacy of the apostolic office, there are found not a few who obstruct its authority, we think that it is completely necessary to assert solemnly the prerogative which the only-begotten Son of God deigned to unite with the supreme pastoral office."

7. The Deputation *de fide* proposes the following formula to the general congregation in place of Suggestions #36 through #75.

"Therefore, faithfully adhering to the tradition received [1195] from the beginning of the Christian religion, for the glory of God our Savior, for the exaltation of the Catholic faith and the salvation of the Christian people, with the approval of the sacred council, we teach and define that it is a divinely revealed dogma that the Roman Pontiff, when he speaks *ex cathedra*, i.e., when exercising his office as pastor and teacher of all Christians he defines, by his supreme apostolic authority, a doctrine of faith or morals which must be held by the universal Church, enjoys, through the divine assistance, that infallibility promised to him in blessed Peter and with which the divine Redeemer wanted His Church to be endowed in defining doctrine of faith or morals; and therefore that the definitions of the same Roman Pontiff are irreformable of themselves."

Chapter Four as Promulgated by Vatican Council I

Moreover in the apostolic primacy which the Roman [1333] Pontiff holds in the universal Church as successor of Peter, the Prince of the Apostles, there is also included the supreme power of teaching. This Holy See has always held this [truth], the perpetual usage of the Church approves it, and the ecumenical Councils, especially those in which the East has come together with the West in a union of faith and charity, have taught it. For the bishops of the Fourth Council of Constantinople, adhering to the footsteps of their predecessors, issued this solemn profession: "The first thing required for salvation is to preserve the rule of the true faith. And because it is not possible to set aside the words of Our Lord Jesus Christ when He says, 'You are Peter and on this rock I will build my Church,' we see that these words are proved true by events, because the Catholic faith has always been preserved immaculate in the Apostolic See and its teaching kept holy. Therefore, desiring to be separated in no way from this faith and teaching, we hope that we may deserve to be in the one communion which the Apostolic See preaches, in which [See] there is present the whole and true security of the Christian religion." Indeed, with the approval of the Second Council of Lyons, the Greeks professed: "The Holy Roman Church holds the supreme and full primacy and power over the universal Catholic Church. She humbly and truly recognizes that she has received this from the Lord Himself in Blessed Peter, the Prince or head of the Apostles, whose successor is the Roman Pontiff; and since, before all others, she is held to defend the truth of the faith, if any questions should arise concerning the faith, they should be defined by her judgment." Finally, the Council of Florence defined: "The Roman Pontiff stands as the true Vicar of Christ, the head of the whole Church and the father and

teacher of all Christians; to him has been given, in Blessed
[1334] Peter, by Our Lord Jesus Christ, the full power of shepherding, ruling and governing the universal Church."

To satisfy this pastoral office, our predecessors always
expended untiring effort to see that the saving doctrine of
Christ be propagated among all the peoples of the earth, and,
with equal care, they watched that it might be preserved pure
and sincere where it had been received. Therefore, the bishops of the whole world, sometimes individually, sometimes
gathered in synods, following the long-established custom of
the Churches and the manner of the ancient rule [of faith]
reported back to this Apostolic See those special dangers
which arose in matters of faith, so that harm to the faith
might be especially repaired in that place where the faith can
suffer no defect. Moreover, the Roman Pontiffs, according to
the dictates of time and circumstances, sometimes by calling
ecumenical councils or asking the opinion of the Church
dispersed throughout the world, sometimes through particular synods, sometimes by using other means which divine
providence supplied, defined those things which must be
held and which they knew, by the help of God, to be consonant with the Sacred Scriptures and apostolic traditions. For
the Holy Spirit promised to the successors of Peter, not that
they would unfold new doctrine which He revealed to them,
but that, with His assistance, they would piously guard and
faithfully expound the revelation or deposit of faith handed
on through the Apostles. All the venerable Fathers and holy
orthodox doctors venerated and followed their [i.e., the successors of Peter] apostolic doctrine; they knew full well that
this See of St. Peter always remained unstained by all error,
according to the divine promise which Our Savior made to
the chief of His disciples when He said, 'I have prayed for
you, that your faith may not fail, and you, having turned,
strengthen your brothers.'

Therefore this charism of truth and unfailing faith was
divinely given to Peter and his successors in this chair so that
they might fulfill their high office for the salvation of all, so
that the whole flock of Christ might, through them, be

turned away from the poisonous food of error and be fed on the food of heavenly doctrine, and so that, the occasion of schism being removed, the whole Church might be preserved as one and, firmly grounded on its foundation, might stand against the gates of hell.

Since in our times, which especially require the salvific efficacy of the apostolic office, there are found not a few who obstruct its authority, we think it is completely necessary to assert solemnly the prerogative which the only-begotten Son of God deigned to unite with the supreme pastoral office.

Therefore, faithfully adhering to the tradition received from the beginning of the Christian religion, for the glory of God our Savior, for the exaltation of the Catholic faith and the salvation of the Christian people, with the approval of the sacred council, we teach and define that it is a divinely revealed dogma that the Roman Pontiff, when he speaks *ex cathedra*, i.e., when exercising his office as pastor and teacher of all Christians he defines, by his supreme apostolic authority, a doctrine of faith or morals which must be held by the universal Church, enjoys, through the divine assistance, that infallibility promised to him in blessed Peter and with which the divine Redeemer wanted His Church to be endowed in defining doctrine of faith or morals; and therefore that the definitions of the same Roman Pontiff are irreformable of themselves and not from the consent of the Church.

"If anyone should presume to contradict this definition of ours—may God prevent that happening—anathema sit."

Relatio of Bishop Vincent Ferrer Gasser on July 11, 1870

Most eminent presidents, eminent and reverend fathers.

I get up to speak today with great sadness and even greater fear. With great sadness, since the treatment of the center of ecclesiastical unity has become the occasion of discord among the reverend fathers, such discord that we are able to say with the prophet: "Seeing this, they will cry out in the streets, and the messengers of peace will weep bitterly" (Is. 33:7). I rise to speak with even greater fear, lest a great cause be ruined by its advocate. Nevertheless, I proceed, counting on divine grace and your good will.

In order that we may pass judgment on each one of the suggestions proposed by the reverend fathers and do so surely and swiftly, it is entirely necessary, first of all, to offer a type of general presentation and then pass on to a particular consideration of each suggested correction. In the general presentation certain principles are to be set up which, once established, will then be of help in passing judgment on the suggested corrections.

As far as the general presentation goes, it consists of two parts as does the Draft which we are discussing. In the first part of this draft we present the arguments for the infallibility of the Roman Pontiff as those arguments are drawn from the public documents [of the Church]; in the second part or paragraph of the Draft we have the definition of infallibility itself. First of all, therefore, we must deal with the arguments presented for the infallibility of the Roman Pontiff.

Since this infallibility is a revealed truth, it should be proved from the fonts of revelation, that is, from Sacred

Scripture and tradition. This matter has been abundantly discussed in the general meetings; nevertheless, certain things remain to be said, at least in passing, so that certain difficulties, raised by some of the fathers, may be removed. Thus, in the first place, let us consider the arguments from Sacred Scripture.

The argument is to be set forth in the following thesis: Christ the Lord granted to St. Peter the prerogative of infallibility in His Church at the same time as He granted him the primacy; this infallibility has passed on—indeed was meant to pass on—to all the successors of St. Peter and heirs of his primacy. Thus, the first part of the thesis is: Christ granted the prerogative of infallibility to St. Peter at the same time He gave him primacy in the universal Church. The places in Sacred Scripture which demonstrate this thesis are very well-known and have been excellently explained by many of the reverend fathers. Enough said on that point. The second part of the thesis is: this prerogative of infallibility has passed, together with the primacy, to the successors of St. Peter and heirs of his primacy. Since many of the reverend fathers have had different opinions on this point, let me offer my opinion briefly. The infallibility granted to St. Peter has passed to all the successors of Peter. The reason for this is the following: the prerogative of infallibility belonged ordinarily to Peter and was inseparably connected with his primacy; hence, it

---

Having introduced his theme, Gasser proceeds to defend the proofs adduced in the proposed Draft as they are found in Scripture and Tradition. His argument from Scripture is summary, as are, indeed, the Scriptural citations in the Draft itself. He presumes that the primacy of the Pope has already been established from Scripture—since that matter was previously treated in chapter three of the Draft which dealt with the primacy. Infallibility, he says, was given to Peter when he received the primacy, and the texts of Scripture which deal with this have, he says, also been previously explained. It simply remains to be demonstrated that infallibility, like the primacy, was intended to be passed to Peter's successors.

passed with the fullness of his apostolic power into the Apostolic See, and to his successors in this See. The same conclusion follows from the famous words of Christ. For as the [1205] words of Christ, "The gates of hell shall not prevail against it" (Mt. 16:16), are not bounded by time but will have authority until the end of the world, so the foundation of the Church on Peter and his successors ought always remain unshaken against the proud gates of those who belong to the nether world, that is against heresies and the builders of heresy, as St. Epiphanius says.

The case was different with the infallibility of the other Apostles; each of them individually was infallible: but this infallibility was extraordinary, granted to them in an extraordinary mode and for an extraordinary purpose, as appears from the words of Christ when He took leave of them before ascending into heaven, saying: "You will receive the power of the Holy Spirit who will come upon you, and you will be my witnesses in Jerusalem, in all Judea, in Samaria, and to the ends of the earth" (Acts 1:8). This promise of the coming Holy Spirit was fulfilled on the day of Pentecost, and, clothed by the Holy Spirit as by power from on high, they began to bear witness to the word of life and to preach in the name of Jesus, "the Lord cooperating with them and confirming their preaching by the signs which accompanied them" (Mk. 16:20).

The office of the Apostles consisted in this: they would be the authentic ocular and auricular witnesses to the word of

---

Peter and all the Apostles, says Gasser, received the gift of infallibility so that they would be able to pass on the revelation they had received free from error and thus securely ground the Church in truth at its very inception. But the gift was given differently to Peter and to the others. Peter received it as something *ordinary*, i.e., personal to him as primate or leader of the Church. The others received it as *extraordinary*, i.e., given for a time as part of an apostolate, which, unlike Peter's primacy, was not going to endure beyond their own lives.

God, witnesses preordained by God and sent by Christ to all nations: and to this office, proper to the Apostles, there was added the corresponding gift of personal infallibility. The bishops succeeded the Apostles not as succeeding to a universal apostolate but rather to an episcopate as rulers of individual churches. And thus it happened that the prerogative of personal infallibility, joined in an extraordinary mode to the apostolate, would not pass on to the bishops. The bishops by power of their office are guardians of the deposit which the Apostles—as witnesses preordained by God—committed to them. It is as Paul says to Timothy: "Hold to the form of sound teaching, which you heard from me in faith and in the love of Christ Jesus. Through the Holy Spirit who dwells in you guard the worthy deposit" (2 Tm. 1:13-14). This same thing is said to all the bishops. In this duty of guarding, communicating and defending the deposit as a treasure of divine truth, the bishops also are helped by the Holy Spirit. But this infallible aid of the Holy Spirit is not present in each of the bishops but rather in the bishops taken together and joined with [their] head, for it was said to all generally and not each individually: "Behold, I am with you all days until the end of time" (Mt. 28:20).

Bishop Gasser, arguing from Scripture again, as the Church has traditionally understood the texts, says that inerrancy was given to Peter so that he would be able to strengthen his brothers in the faith (cf. Lk. 22:31-32). This role of confirming the faith of the others continues in the primacy of Peter's successors and they, therefore, must also inherit the gift of infallibility or inerrancy. This gift, Gasser points out, was one given to the entire Church as well. It is implicit in Christ's promise to be with the Church even to the consummation of the world (cf. Mt. 28:20). As successors of the Apostles and thus, as chief teachers in the Church, the bishops inherit this infallibility, not as individuals but as a collectivity when united with the successor of Peter who, as Bossuet, the bishop of Meaux, pointed out, needed permanence in truth in order to be the center of ecclesiastical unity.

This prerogative granted to St. Peter by the Lord Jesus Christ was supposed to pass to all Peter's successors because the chair of Peter is the center of unity in the Church. But if the Pontiff should fall into an error of faith, the Church would dissolve, deprived of the bond of unity. The bishop of Meaux speaks very well on this point, saying: "If this Roman See could fall and be no longer the See of truth but of error and pestilence, then the Catholic Church herself would not have the bond of a society and would be schismatic and scattered—which in fact is impossible."[1]

Let no one say: "Yes, the See of Peter is the center of unity, but from that there only follows the office which the Roman pastor has of confirming and of preserving his brothers in the faith. But the office is one thing, the authority, especially an infallible authority, is something else." I reply: how would the Roman Pontiff be able to fulfill this office which was divinely and especially given to him if he did not have a special authority which all others—even the bishops whether dispersed throughout the world or gathered together —should recognize as unassailable?   [1206]

The citation of Bossuet is a deft touch since it comes from the talk which the famous bishop gave in response to the congregation which drew up the *Declaration of the French Clergy* in March of 1682 when Louis XIV was combatting the papal claims. This Declaration, following in tone some of the conciliarist decrees of the Council of Constance (especially the *Sacrosancta* of April, 1415), held, in its fourth article (to be cited by Gasser later in his relatio) that the Pope has the chief role when it comes to matters of faith, but that, nonetheless, his decisions needed confirmation by the judgment of the entire Church. This position is, in essence, the thesis of *Gallicanism* which, in one form or another, perdured into the nineteenth century and which was ever in the background—and sometimes in the foreground—of the discussions on primacy and papal infallibility at Vatican Council I.

Working from the citation of Bossuet, Bishop Gasser argues that it would be impossible for the successor of Peter to fulfill his task of confirming the other bishops in the faith if a perma-

Let no one say: "Indeed, in order that the Roman Pontiff be able to fulfill his office he should have authority over all the bishops, but there is no necessity that this authority be in itself infallible. It is sufficient that it be infallible along with the other bishops." But I respond: as is true in the case of the center of unity in the heavenly bodies, so too the center of unity in the Church of Christ under the heavens should act with a continual and permanent unchallengeable authority. If the authority of the Pope were not unchallengeable in itself but only [when exercised] together with the bishops, then, by divine law, the Pope should have delegates of the entire episcopate to assist him—delegates who would represent that episcopate by divine law. But Christ instituted nothing of this sort; rather He placed Peter and his successor as an immobile bulwark of faith, as the heir of a confirmed faith and as the one who confirms his brothers, and, finally, as the pastor of the whole flock of the Lord, ruling it in such a way that it lacks nothing and leading it to good pastures. That the infallibility granted to Peter was to have passed to his successors is also proved—to use the words of Cardinal Cajetan—from the fact that when the Pope makes a judicial and definitive decision determining that something is heresy and that it must be held as such by the Church then it is clear that we are all bound to accept his decision and that whoever pertinaciously clings to the opposite view is considered a heretic.

---

nent guarantee of inerrancy had not been given to those who would succeed Peter in his Chair. It is a gift that cannot be dependent on the consent of the other bishops since such a consent would ultimately nullify the special duty of the primate to strengthen the others when their own faith was weak. In effect, Gasser is citing Bossuet here as a witness to the general tradition of the Church, and he goes on to add to the witness of Bossuet testimonies drawn from Thomas De Vio, Cardinal Cajetan (1469-1534), the great commentator on St. Thomas Aquinas; and from Melchior Cano (1509-1560), one of the great theologians from the period of the Protestant Reformation and the Council of Trent.

Therefore the whole Church is able to err, following the decision of a Pope, if the Pope in such a definition is able to err. Therefore it must be believed that the promise of Christ made to the Church, viz., "The Holy Spirit will teach you all truth" (Jn. 16:18), is fulfilled through one with no more difficulty than through a multitude, thus preserving the divine order which governs the lower through the higher and the higher through the uppermost. Thus Cajetan.[2] And Melchior Cano dares to add: "Whoever would deny that the power of binding and loosing which Christ is believed to have given to St. Peter is now present in the Bishop of Rome, such a person (i.e., one who would deny this power) is lawfully and rightly held to be a heretic. Whoever would deny to those who have succeeded Peter the strength of Peter for confirming his brothers must be judged to be heretical."[3] We now come to the arguments from tradition, and this is the argument from the public documents of the councils which can be found in the proposed Draft itself. However, before I make a few reflections on these documents, let me say a little bit in a general way about the argument from tradition as it is brought forth to prove the infallibility of the Roman Pontiff. Generally speaking the argument comes from tradition but it can be construed in different ways. Let me say it as I will (for now I will omit things for the sake of time); let me say how I would construct this argument from tradition and the way I was led to use this method.

The argument from Tradition as it is found in the Draft is basically confined to the citations drawn from three ecumenical councils of the Church: Constantinople IV (869-870), Lyons (1274), and Florence (1438-1445). Before giving an explanation of these citations as they appear in context, Bishop Gasser outlines a general argument from Tradition, one that he personalizes by indicating that the reflections came to him one day as he was praying at the *confessio,* i.e., the area just in front of the main altar of St. Peter's Basilica. He argues from a fact to the reason for that fact. The fact is: the Roman See, in the person of its bishops, has strenuously and at great cost defended the

One day when I was praying on my knees at the *confessio* of St. Peter's, I lifted up my eyes and saw the words inscribed there which say: "From this place one faith shines on the world." At these words I recalled all those things which, from the earliest ages of the Christian religion down to our own day, the holy Apostolic See has done and suffered in order to preserve the authority of the faith in the Church of Christ and to repair that authority where it has been harmed. While I was thinking about this, the deep conviction held me that the Holy See would not have been able to fight so strenuously, so constantly and so successfully for the truth unless it had always been persuaded of the gift of inerrancy, promised, in the person of Peter, to Peter's successors, and unless the Church had offered its assent to this conviction of the Holy [1207] See. Thus, most reverend and eminent fathers, the traditional argument which I want to present to you. As I have already said, I now abstain from proposing it. In order to strengthen the first part of this argument, I read again and again the genuine epistles of the Roman Pontiffs as edited by Coustantio and by Andrea Thiel, his recent continuator. As often as I read them and the more I considered them, the more did I become convinced that the Roman Pontiffs, as they descended into the arena as witnesses, doctors and judges of the universal Church to fight for the Christian truth, were incapable of erring, through the power of a divine promise.

Church Universal against heresy. The reason for the Roman Church's assumption of the role of defender of the Faith has been its own awareness that Christ had promised to that See, in the person of Peter and his successors, the gift of inerrancy. This inerrancy indeed was a gift that the Roman See, through its bishops, claimed for itself. And the local Churches, by their own manner of acting, implicitly or explicitly, have assented to the claims made by the See of Rome in the person of its bishops. Thus, one finds agreement of the Church Universal to the claims of the Diocese of Rome, in the person of its Bishop, to infallibility.

Don't let anyone say that the Roman Pontiffs, commending the dignity of their own See, speaking, that is, on their own behalf, should not be believed. For if the testimony of the Roman Pontiffs is weakened for that reason [viz., because they speak on their own behalf], then indeed the entire ecclesiastical hierarchy is called into question: the authority of the teaching Church is not able to be proved except through the teaching Church.

As far as the second part of the traditional argument is concerned, viz., the assent of the Church which is offered to the faith of the Roman Pontiffs concerning the gift of inerrancy of their See, the Church has well manifested this assent indirectly (i.e., by reason of its mode of acting) as well as directly and by explicit words. Passing over in silence the explicit testimonies by which the holy Fathers and the councils have manifested their assent, I ought to spend a little time on the indirect testimony which is drawn from the Church's mode of acting, since doing so will offer me the opportunity of removing some of the difficulties which have been raised by some of the reverend fathers. This indirect testimony rises from the rule of faith which the most ancient Fathers have handed down.

Concluding his personal reflection on the argument from tradition, Gasser answers the possible objection which would claim that, in pressing its own claims, the Roman See is not an objective witness to Tradition. His answer is to the effect that the only way we can determine what the Church understands about her own constitution is to examine what she says about herself. In this case what the Roman See has said about itself in putting forth its own claim to infallibility has been assented to by the local Churches and is, thus, the teaching of the Church Universal which is inerrant in matters of faith.

In light of what he will proceed to say about papal infallibility not requiring any juridical consent or assent of the Church Universal, Gasser's argument may appear incongruent or even amazing. The Church, he says, has assented to the claims of the Roman See and the Church cannot err. Therefore the claims of the Roman See to be infallible are part of the normative tradi-

As you know, St. Irenaeus, who established the rule of faith as being the consensus of those Churches which were founded by Apostles, simultaneously established a more compendious and more secure rule, viz., the tradition of the Roman Church, with which, because of its more powerful primacy in the Church, all the faithful throughout the world should agree and in which the apostolic tradition is preserved by all the faithful from everywhere, as they live in communion with the Roman Church as the center of unity. Therefore, according to St. Irenaeus, the faith of the Roman Church is, because of the dignity of its primacy, normative for all the other Churches, and, because of its dignity as center, the principle of preservation for the other Churches.

St. Augustine proposes the same rule of faith in the following words: "If indeed one considers the order of episcopal succession, what more certain and salvific than the one listed as coming from Peter himself, to whom, as bearing the figure of the whole Church, the Lord said: 'On this rock I will build my Church, and the gates of hell shall not conquer it.' Linus succeeded Peter...and so down to the present Pontiff. In this line of succession no Donatist was bishop."[4] For Augustine this was enough to damn the Donatist heresy, that fact that no bishop of the Romans was a Donatist; and this

---

tion of the Church. For Gasser, however, the assent is not the reason for the rightness of Rome's claims, but a witness to their truth.

The text from St. Irenaeus, cited several times directly or indirectly by Gasser, is from the *Adversus Haereses,* book III, 3. A recent work by a non-Catholic translates it as follows: "For every church must be in harmony with this Church because of its outstanding pre-eminence *[propter potentiorem principalitatem]*, that is, the faithful from everywhere, since the apostolic tradition is preserved in it by those from everywhere" (trans. by Edward Rochie Hardy in C. Richardson (ed.), *Early Christian Fathers,* The Macmillan Co., N.Y., 1970, p. 372). The *potentiorem principalitatem* is a crux for translators and interpreters.

rule, because of the authority of Peter, Augustine calls more secure and salvific. This same assent to the faith of the Roman Pontiffs in their own inerrancy has been sufficiently manifested by the Church in that it has always held communion with the Holy See as completely and absolutely necessary. Communion with the chair of Peter was, and was considered to be, communion with the Church and with Peter himself, and indeed was even compared with the truth revealed by Christ. "I do not know Vitalis," writes Jerome, "Melitus I reject, Paulinus I ignore. Whoever does not gather with you (that is, with Pope Damasus) scatters; that is, whoever does not belong to Christ belongs to the antichrist."[5] [1208] Furthermore, because the testimony which the Church offered to the faith of the Roman Pontiffs concerning the inerrancy of their own See is certain, the holy Fathers held it as certain and obvious that Peter, constituted the foundation of the Church, could not be separated from the Church itself and that the Church could not be separated from Christ and that Christ could not be separated from the truth. Because of this, St. Ambrose says very beautifully: "Peter is he to whom the Lord said: 'You are Peter, and on this rock I will build the Church.' Therefore where Peter is, there is the Church; where the Church is, there is no death but only eternal life. And therefore Christ added: 'And the gates of hell shall not prevail, and I will give you the keys of the kingdom of heaven.'"[6]

The Patristic texts adduced by Bishop Gasser can hardly be taken as clear indications of their authors' belief in the infallibility of the Pope as Vatican Council I was going to define it. Gasser himself has indicated that the statements of the Fathers which he has brought forth fall under the category of "indirect testimony" (p. 27 above)—a testimony which gives evidence of a "rule of faith" which existed for the writers of the ancient Church. This rule of faith was essentially this: unity with the See of Peter was the most certain guarantee available that one was walking in the way of the true faith.

The thrust of his argument is a familiar one to all who study the development of doctrine: aspects of the Faith are lived in

This assent to the faith of the Roman Pontiffs concerning the inerrancy of their own See has also been offered by the Church inasmuch as every doctrine, when it has first been damned as alien to the Faith and profane by the Roman Pontiff, is also rejected by all who are truly faithful. "How will Italy receive," says Jerome, "what Rome has condemned? How will the bishops receive what the Apostolic See has damned?"[7] Finally we are able to prove the same assent to the faith of the Roman Pontiffs concerning the inerrancy of their own See from the fact that, in all cases involving matters of Faith, recourse was had to the Apostolic See—recourse, indeed, as if to the authority of Peter and Paul—and also from the fact that an appeal against the Roman See and the dogmatic definitions of this See was never licit.

I will refrain from bringing forth what pertains to direct testimony or to explicit words of the Holy Fathers. But I should respond to some objections which are very frequently made against these testimonies.

---

practice before they are formulated explicitly or even adequately. This can be seen, for example, in the case of the baptism of infants. There is evidence that it was practiced in the Church from earliest times. Only gradually, however, were the reasons for the practice articulated—and then not adequately until the time of Augustine's writings on grace and original sin against the Pelagians. So, too, by analogy, in the case of pontifical infallibility; need for unity with the See of Peter is seen as a fact, is commented upon by the early writers, is attributed to the unique place of the Petrine See, is associated with its unblemished adherence to the correct faith, etc. Only the passage of time enabled the Church of Rome and the other Churches to articulate the reasons for that which the entire Church experienced in practice. As Gasser has noted, this articulation was frequently the work of the Bishops of Rome themselves—an articulation then assented to or accepted by the other Churches.

The early tentative attempts to articulate the lived-experience of the Church can be frustrating to the theologian and historian who often would like to find a clarity of statement which in fact could only be expected at a later time.

It has been stated that the texts of tradition which are brought forth by the defenders of infallibility are mutilated, falsified, interpolated or spurious or prove nothing more than the primacy. Harsh words those! But let this be said: what is proved thereby? Can it really be denied that there exist testimonies by which the special gift of the infallibility of the Roman Pontiff is proved or that these testimonies are completely certain, either by looking at the immediate force of the words or at the context and purpose of the work in question?

It has been said by some of the very reverend speakers that an infallibility of the Roman Pontiff which is personal, separate and absolute is not proved by these testimonies. Whatever is to be said concerning these qualifiers—about which I shall presently speak—let me say this: it has often been said, but as far as I can see, never been proved, that according to the mind of the Holy Fathers, the efficient cause of the infallibility of the Roman Pontiff is something other than the protection of Christ and the assistance of the Holy Spirit as promised to Peter for all ages, or that the consent of the Church is a condition *de jure* without which the dogmatic judgments of the Roman Pontiff could not be infallible. Can it really be said that the Fathers at Chalcedon, before they hailed the Tome of St. Leo to Flavian as having come from the mouth of Peter, anxiously inquired as to whether this Tome adhered to the advice of the bishops? Even more, can it really be said that history, which tells us so many wonderful things about the origin of this Tome, makes mention of the consent of the bishops which preceded this dogmatic defini-tion of the Roman Pontiff?

Having cited the acclamation given by the bishops at Chal-cedon (451) to Pope Leo's *Tome to Flavian* as a testimony to the Church's recognition of the Roman Church's authority in teach-ing on matters of faith, Gasser moves on to treat directly the Draft's own presentation of the argument from Tradition, viz., the ecumenical councils of Constantinople, Lyons, and Florence. These three councils were chosen deliberately because the

Now I come to the arguments of tradition which are set forth in the proposed chapter itself, come, that is, to the documents adduced from three councils. As far as these arguments are concerned, they are drawn, as you know, from the ecumenical councils in which—after there had, unfortunately, been schisms between the Eastern and Western Church—the East and West came together to remove this schism. Since many objections have been brought forward in the general [1209] congregations with the purpose of weakening the probative force which is contained in these testimonies, it is necessary to review a few things.

As far as the Council of Constantinople IV is concerned, the words adduced in the proposed chapter are almost identical with the formula of Pope Hormisdas, by which the Acacian schism was resolved, and which was approved not only by the Church of the West but also by a very large part of the

---

Churches of the East participated in all three of them and because the documents which came forth from them give strong testimony to the claims of the Roman See. It has often been noted that the bishops of the East were under a great deal of pressure, from the emperors and, later, from the threat of Moslem invasion, to achieve doctrinal harmony with Rome and the West. It is noted, too, that the dogmatic harmony achieved at Lyons and Florence did not last. Undoubtedly, in each case, the pressures were real, but it is also true that no bishop was forced to sign the decrees of the Councils and that, in fact, some Eastern bishops did not sign the decrees to which the majority of bishops gave their approval. It is also undoubtedly true that some (many?) of the Eastern bishops who did approve the conciliar decrees—and the great majority of them did approve—were not fully happy with each and every aspect of the final decrees. Nonetheless, to argue that they signed only out of compulsion or fear and therefore signed while not really believing what they were teaching by the decrees of those same councils—or believed only in part—is to level against the bishops of the East a totally unwarranted charge of mass hypocrisy.

As Gasser indicates, the Council of Constantinople IV (869-870) incorporated into its final decree the Formula of

Eastern Church. It was said that this formula contains nothing more than the confidence that there would never happen to the Chair of Peter what had already regretfully happened to so many other Apostolic Sees, and that the successors of the Prince of the Apostles would function until the end of the world in the task of protecting the Faith and of confirming their brothers.

But this interpretation does not agree with either the literal or the historical meaning of the document in question. It does not agree with the letter because the words of this formula of Pope Hormisdas, which were received almost verbatim by the Council of Constantinople IV, say, as you know, the following: "The first thing required for salvation is to keep the norm of correct faith and to deviate in no way from what the Fathers have established, because it is not possible to lay aside the words of our Lord Jesus Christ who said, 'You are Peter, and on this rock I will build my Church.' These words are proved true by their effects because, in the Apostolic See, the Catholic religion has always been preserved immaculate. Desiring in no way to be separated from

---

Pope Hormisdas. Hormisdas was bishop of Rome from 514 to 523. Previous to his pontificate, relations with the East had been ruptured by the Acacian Schism (484-519). Acacius, the patriarch of Constantinople, in a doctrinal statement called the Henoticon, had called into question the decrees of the Council of Chalcedon concerning the two natures in the one Person of Christ. Pope Felix III excommunicated Acacius in 484. Relations between the Churches of Rome and Constantinople were restored when a successor of Acacius, Patriarch John, accepted the doctrinal Formula of Pope St. Hormisdas in 519. The Formula contained some very explicit language on the prerogatives of the Roman See, and it is Constantinople IV's repetition of that same language which Gasser explains and defends as an appropriate witness to papal infallibility. The appropriateness of the Hormisdas Formula to the work of Constantinople IV is made apparent when one remembers that Constantinople IV dealt with putting an end to the Photian schism and with establishing the norm of faith for the Church Universal.

this hope and faith and following in all things what has been established by the Fathers, we anathematize all heretics, etc." And at the end it is said: "Therefore, as we have said before, following the Apostolic See in all things and preaching all things determined by it, I hope that I may merit to be in one communion with you (i.e., with Pope Hormisdas) and with what the Apostolic See preaches, in which See [resides] the integral and true solidity of the Christian religion." These are the words of Hormisdas' formula.

As far as the meaning of this formula is concerned, the manifest sense of these words is the following: in order that the East, which has been cut off from the Apostolic See, might again receive communion with that same Apostolic See and with the Catholic Church, the bishops should issue a solemn profession of faith concerning the prerogative of the Apostolic See; they should, that is, guard the rule of right faith, if in hope and faith we firmly hold that the promise of Our Lord Jesus Christ to Peter is not able to be laid aside, something indeed proved from the course of events themselves, in the fact, namely, that the true religion has always been preserved unblemished in the Apostolic See. Against the testimony drawn from the Council of Lyons it was said that this testimony was neither used nor approved by the Council. So that I will not end up repeating what the relator of chapter three has already said on this matter, I will make only a few points on one item, the one, namely, which attempts to show that this formula of faith was not used by the Council of Lyons because the formula itself was never discussed in the Council. The fact that it was not discussed is indeed true but that fact doesn't prove anything against the authority of this document: on the contrary the authority of the document is further strengthened. The reason for the lack of discussion of this profession of faith by the Council of Lyons was none other than the fact that, in this case, they were not treating something new nor something never spoken of, but rather something, insofar as it referred to the primacy of the Roman Pontiff, already long since approved in the Council of Constantinople IV for the universal Church at the time of Pope Hormisdas, and something about which there was no doubt among the Latins.

That this was the reason for omitting the discussion is clear from the letter which Pope Clement IV sent to the Emperor Michael Palaeologus and with which he transmitted the same formula which would afterwards be read in the Second Council of Lyons. For, when the Emperor communicated to Clement IV his plan of convoking a council in the East in order to decide the dispute in that manner, the Pope [1210] responded with these words: "Indeed the prescribed truth of the orthodox faith is pure, certain and solid and consonant with the teaching of the Gospel and it has been affirmed by the Holy Fathers and by the definition of the Roman Pontiffs in their synods. Since it is not fitting, we do not want to submit this matter to new discussion or definition as if, by such discussion, we were calling into doubt this truth in any way, thereby going against what is right and permitted. And therefore, although in what you have written (i.e, in the letter of the Emperor) you treat of the convocation of a council and although you (i.e., the Emperor), through said letters, ask that a council be convoked in your land, we, nevertheless, have no intention of calling a council for a discussion or definition of this type. This decision does not mean that we fear any man nor that we fear that the Roman Church will be overcome by the prudence of the Greeks, but because it would be completely unfitting—what is more, even non-necessary and illegal—to call into doubt the prescribed purity of the true faith, affirmed by so many authorities on Scripture, fortified by the opinions of so many holy men and by the firm definition of the Roman Pontiffs. For the defense of this truth, if it were necessary, we ought to be ready to undergo martyrdom and even give our body to be exposed to death."[58] Thus Clement. And so it is not to be wondered at that Gregory X also did not permit a discussion of this formula at the Council of Lyons. The third document is taken from the Council of Florence. It has been said that, of those things which are brought forth in our proposed chapter from the Council of Florence, there is nothing in them which a sober interpreter can use to establish the doctrine of infallibility. But it is clear that the mind of the fathers at Florence was far different and this can be seen from the commentary which Bro. John made before Pope Eugene IV and the Emperor John Palaeologus in order that the Emperor might know what the meaning of the formula was which treated of the Roman Pontiff. And so, treating each part of the formula individually, he explained the part of the formula which reads, *The Roman Pontiff stands as head of the whole Church and the father and teacher of all Christians,* by saying: "Since all Christians agree and should agree with one another in the faith, he (the Roman Pontiff) is placed as the teacher of unblemished faith because of the privilege granted to Peter." Explaining the part which reads, *To that same See and to the Roman Pontiff there was given in the Blessed Prince of the Apostles the full power of feeding, ruling and governing the universal Church,* Bro. John drew upon the letter of Pope St. Agatho to the Emperor Constantine IV in respect to the third Council of Constantinople, and from that letter drew the following conclusion: "In this authority (i.e., Agatho), these following three things are clearly asserted. First, that the feeding of all the flock is committed to Peter and to his successors. Second, that the Apostolic See has never fallen into any part of error, but has always remained unblemished in faith. Third, that so great is the authority of the Apostolic See that the Church Universal and the general councils have always faithfully followed its apostolic teaching, and the Catholic Fathers have always accepted that same doctrine, and that the words *(that your faith may not fail)* are understood of the Apostolic See to mean that it is immune from error and that the confirmation of all the brothers who are wavering in faith pertains to the same See and to the Roman Pontiff."[9] Thus was this matter explained in the very Council of Florence itself, and this must be held as its authentic meaning since it was deliberately proposed this way by the order of the Roman Pontiff so that the [1211] Emperor might understand the meaning of the formula.

From all that has been said it is manifestly clear that when we bring forth the definition of Florence in order to establish the infallibility of the Roman Pontiff we are, in no way, supposing an alien sense for the words, but are truly interpreting them according to the mind of the fathers at Florence. It is clear as well that the word "hence" which connects the first part of the chapter with the second by way of drawing a conclusion and which has been criticized by many speakers nonetheless occupies its rightful place.

Before I conclude the relatio concerning this first part of our proposed chapter, i.e, about the arguments for pontifical infallibility, let me offer my opinion about the very grave objection which has frequently been brought forth in these general congregations, viz., that having once promulgated the infallibility of the Roman Pontiff the divine constitution of the Church would have been changed. Why?

It has been said that henceforth general councils would no longer be necessary. I answer: they will be necessary in the future as they were necessary in the past. They were never absolutely necessary if what you are talking of is only a matter of Christians of good will knowing the truth with certitude. For they were able to know the truth through the ordinary magisterium of the Church, that is, through the bishops having communion with the Apostolic See: for where the Church is, there is the Spirit of God, and where the Spirit of God is, there is truth. Every grace is from the Spirit and the Spirit is truth, says St. Irenaeus. They were able to know the truth from the solemn dogmatic definitions of the Roman Pontiff. Augustine said to Julian, "Why do you still seek to examine that which has already been decided by the Apostolic See?"[10] clearly indicating by these words that,

---

The "hence" to which Gasser refers can be found by looking at the beginning of the second paragraph of the Draft. It was subsequently replaced when the corrections proposed on July 9 were incorporated into the Draft. The first words of the insertion, however, contain the same sense of drawing a conclusion from what has preceded.

once a decision of the Apostolic See has been given, there is already present a certain and unshakeable witness to the truth, as long as there is present the good will to submit oneself to it. Therefore general councils were not necessary in order to know the truth, but in order to repress errors. Since errors were flourishing in such a way that the Christian commonwealth was in a certain way endangered, the Catholic Church opposed to them its most solemn judgment through a general council. But the most solemn judgment of the Church in matters of faith and morals is and always will be the judgment of an ecumenical council, in which the Pope passes judgment together with the bishops of the Catholic world who meet and judge together with him. But some go on to say that general councils in the future will not be free; the bishops will no longer be true judges. I reply: they will be free as they were free in past times. For even future councils will be held in such a way that, as far as the things to be treated in the council are concerned, there will either have been no previous dogmatic definition of the Roman Pontiff or there will have been a previous dogmatic definition. In the first case, if the Pope leaves to the council all the propositions to be fully treated, the council will be able to use its full liberty in the Lord; in the second case, the council will do all that which past general councils have done in a similar situation. Let Constantinople III, in its manner of dealing with the dogmatic epistle of Pope Agatho, serve as an example. The first seven sessions of this council were concerned with certain preambles, that is, with the reading of the documents which concerned the Council. At the end of the seven sessions the legates of the Roman Pontiff requested that the conciliar fathers declare whether they agreed with the sugges-

---

Having defended the testimony adduced from the three ecumenical councils, and before proceeding to comment on the second part of the Draft, i.e., on the definition of infallibility itself, Bishop Gasser attempted to answer an objection frequently leveled against the definition of papal infallibility. That objection stated that, once having defined the infallibility of the

tion or epistle of Agatho. This declaration was set before
the next session. And thus in the eighth session the conciliar
fathers declared, "Just as the suggestions of the most holy [1212]
Pope of Ancient Rome hold, so, O Lord (saying this as they
faced the Emperor), do I profess and believe."[11] Therefore this
declaration was certainly nothing other than a judgment of
true and faithful adherence. Indeed, when Macarius of Anti-
och, who afterwards pertinaciously contradicted the definitions of the Council, did not acquiesce in those definitions,
the conciliar fathers, in order to satisfy all doubts, permitted
him and his followers to defend their opinion by bringing
forth the testimonies of the Fathers. These testimonies, sub-
jected to an examination and judgment, were found to be
partly spurious and partly mutilated and were then rejected
by the Council. To them were opposed the testimony of
Sacred Scripture and of the Fathers which were appended to
the epistle of Pope Agatho. These also were submitted to a
study with all the best codices [of the Fathers]. When all
these appeared in clear light as being integral, authentic and
probative, the Council arrived at its synodal definition concerning the twofold will and operation of Christ. In this definition, as the holy synod expressly states, the epistle of Pope
Agatho is again set before their eyes as the living norm. In

Pope, there would never be need again for an ecumenical council. Living as we do after the celebration of a Second Vatican
Council, the objection seems to carry little weight, and, indeed,
history has demonstrated that Gasser's reply was accurate. He
said, in essence: papal infallibility is not a new doctrine; the
Pope has always been infallible. We are simply about to define
that truth. And, although the Pope has always been infallible,
ecumenical councils were held in the past and so will they be in
the future. They have never been, he says, *absolutely* necessary,
but they have always been the "most solemn judgment" of the
Church in matters of faith and morals, since they visibly manifest
the union of the Pope with the other bishops in fulfilling their
roles as teachers of the faith. As such, ecumenical councils will
always remain necessary.

this way, therefore, the holy synod, in a solemn judgment, reconciled the obedience due the Roman Pontiff with its own liberty "so that (as the words of Leo concerning the Council of Chalcedon say) what was first formulated by the First See, the judgment of the entire Christian world might receive as having come forth from them, so that, in this also, the members might be in harmony with the head."[12] In this harmony of the members with the head there clearly shines forth the assistance of the Holy Spirit as promised to the Church. Thus did the sixth holy synod act, and all the others have acted in the same way.

I now come to the second part of our proposed chapter, that is, to the definition of papal infallibility itself. This is contained in the second part of chapter four. In the general relatio on this second part, it seems to me that two things are necessary: 1. to determine accurately the state of the question, and, 2. to illustrate the formula of the definition by a brief commentary. First of all, therefore, the state of the question.

When we attempt a more accurate determination of the state of the question, we first come upon the words which have already so many times been ordered into exile from this hall, but which have not yet gone into exile. Those words are: infallibility which is *personal, separate,* and *absolute.* In reality the question hinges on these words. Let us see, therefore, as briefly as possible, what the sense of these words is.

As he indicated earlier that he would do, Gasser now proceeds to explain in what sense the words "personal," "separate," and "absolute" may be applied to the infallibility of the Pope. He here enters upon one of the more important sections of his entire relatio, for with this explanation he begins to delineate the parameters of papal infallibility. He will return to this theme later, as well, when he gives the official explanation of the Deputation's proposed new formula or wording for the definition itself (cf. texts, pp. 12-13).

The words "personal," "separate," and "absolute" do not appear either in the Draft or in the final form of Chapter Four

1. In what sense can the infallibility of the Roman Pontiff be said to be *personal*? It is said to be *personal* in order to exclude in this way a distinction between the Roman Pontiff and the Roman Church. Indeed, infallibility is said to be personal in order thereby to exclude a distinction between the See and the one who holds the See. Since this distinction did not acquire any patrons in the general congregations, I shall refrain from saying anything about it. Therefore, having rejected the distinction between the Roman Church and the Roman Pontiff, between the See and the possessor of the See, that is, between the universal series and the individual Roman Pontiffs succeeding each other in this series, we defend the personal infallibility of the Roman Pontiff inasmuch as this prerogative belongs, by the promise of Christ, to each and every legitimate successor of Peter in his chair.

Having said this, the notion of papal infallibility is not yet sufficiently defined. The personal infallibility of the Pope must be more accurately defined in itself in the following way: it does not belong to the Roman Pontiff inasmuch as he is a private person, nor even inasmuch as he is a private teacher, since, as such, he is equal with all other private teachers and, as Cajetan wisely noted, equal does not have power over equal, not such power as the Roman Pontiff exercises [1213] over the Church Universal. Hence we do not speak about personal infallibility, although we do defend the infallibility of the person of the Roman Pontiff, not as an individual person

---

of *Pastor Aeternus*. And with reason, as Gasser indicates. Although capable of a proper interpretation and, indeed, true to some extent, they can be so interpreted as to isolate papal infallibility from the Church herself, something which, as Gasser maintains, is contrary to the very reason for the existence of the papal prerogative as willed by Christ.

Gasser first clarifies the word "personal." Papal infallibility is personal, he says, in the sense that it belongs to the individual who is Bishop of the Roman Church, and not just to the Roman

but as the person of the Roman Pontiff or a public person, that is, as head of the Church in his relation to the Church Universal. Indeed it should not be said that the Pontiff is infallible simply because of the authority of the papacy but rather inasmuch as he is certainly and undoubtedly subject to the direction of divine assistance. By the authority of the papacy, the Pontiff is always the supreme judge in matters of faith and morals, and the father and teacher of all Christians. But the divine assistance promised to him, by which he cannot err, he only enjoys as such when he really and actually exercises his duty as supreme judge and universal teacher of the Church in disputes about the Faith. Thus, the sentence "The Roman Pontiff is infallible" should not be treated as false, since Christ promised that infallibility to the person of Peter and his successors, but it is incomplete since the Pope is only infallible when, by a solemn judgment, he defines a matter of faith and morals for the Church universal.

2. In what sense can the infallibility of the Pope be said to be *separate*? It is able to be called *separate*, or rather distinct because it rests on a special promise of Christ and therefore on a special assistance of the Holy Spirit, which assistance is not one and the same with that which the whole body of the teaching Church enjoys when united with its head. For since Peter and his successor are the center of ecclesiastical unity, whose task it is to preserve the Church in a unity of faith and

---

Church in general, as if one could distinguish between the Roman Church and its Bishop in this regard. It is not personal, however, if, by that, one means that the Pope receives the gift as a private person, as just one individual among many. The gift pertains to the Pontiff as a public person, i.e., as Bishop of Rome and visible head of the Church, and then only when he is defining a matter of faith or morals for the entire Church. This gift, furthermore, does not flow directly from the Pope's authority as Pope, for then he would always be exercising the gift, but comes from a special divine assistance given to him when, in act, he is fulfilling his role as supreme teacher in a definitively binding manner.

charity and to repair the Church when disturbed, his condition and his relation to the Church are completely special; and to this special and distinct condition corresponds a special and distinct privilege. Therefore, in this sense there belongs to the Roman Pontiff a separate infallibility. But in saying this we do not separate the Pontiff from his ordained union with the Church. For the Pope is only infallible when, exercising his function as teacher of all Christians and therefore representing the whole Church, he judges and defines what must be believed or rejected by all. He is no more able to be separated from the universal Church than the foundation from the building it is destined to support. Indeed we do not separate the Pope, defining, from the cooperation and consent of the Church, at least in the sense that we do not exclude this cooperation and this consent of the Church. This is clear from the purpose for which this prerogative has been divinely granted.

The purpose of this prerogative is the preservation of truth in the Church. The special exercise of this prerogative occurs when there arise somewhere in the Church scandals against the faith, i.e., dissensions and heresies which the bishops of the individual churches or even gathered together in provincial council are unable to repress so that they are forced to appeal to the Apostolic See regarding the case, or when the bishops themselves are infected by the sad stain of error. And thereby we do not exclude the cooperation of the Church because the infallibility of the Roman Pontiff does not come to him in the manner of inspiration or of revelation but through a divine assistance. Therefore the Pope, by reason of his office and the gravity of the matter, is held to use the means suitable for properly discerning and aptly enunciating the truth. These means are councils, or the advice of the bishops, cardinals, theologians, etc. Indeed, the means are diverse according to the diversity of situations, and we should piously believe that, in the divine assistance promised to Peter and his successors by Christ, there is simultaneously contained a promise about the means which are necessary and suitable to make an infallible pontifical judgment.

Finally we do not separate the Pope, even minimally, [1214] from the consent of the Church, as long as that consent is not laid down as a condition which is either antecedent or consequent. We are not able to separate the Pope from the consent of the Church because this consent is never able to be lacking to him. Indeed, since we believe that the Pope is infallible through the divine assistance, by that very fact we also believe that the assent of the Church will not be lacking to his definitions since it is not able to happen that the body of bishops be separated from its head, and since the Church universal is not able to fail. For it is impossible that general

---

In a sense, says Gasser, papal infallibility may be called "separate" since it is given by a special promise of Christ, produced by a special aid of the Holy Spirit and given to one who serves a unique role in the Church. As such it is not identical with the gift of indefectability and infallibility in truth promised to the entire Church. Having said all that, however, Gasser is insistent in pointing out all the ways that papal infallibility is not "separate," insofar as it is not apart from, or opposed to, or set over against the entire Church.

The Pope can teach infallibly because he receives the gift of inerrancy as chief teacher of the Church when he is defining a truth of faith or morals for the entire Church. Furthermore, the cooperation and assent of the Church is always an aspect of papal infallibility. The Pope is morally bound to use all appropriate means for ascertaining revealed truth, among which is the seeking of prudent advice from whatever source necessary. This moral necessity for seeking counsel comes, in part, from the fact that infallibility does not work by way of divine inspiration. This remark of Gasser, means—to put it in the rather crude terminology often used in polemics—that the Pope has "no pipeline to heaven." It is rather a divine assistance which guarantees that, after consultation, study, and prayer, he will never make a mistake when he definitively proposes a truth to be believed by the entire Church, or definitively rejects an error as something that must not be held by the Church. The consent of the Church will always be present to such teaching since it is the same Spirit who gives the gift of infallibility for the sake of the truth and sees to it that the Church welcomes such truth.

obscurity be spread in respect to the more important truths which touch upon religion, as the Synod of Pistoia held.

3. Note well. It is asked in what sense the infallibility of the Roman Pontiff is *absolute*. I reply and openly admit: in no sense is pontifical infallibility absolute, because absolute infallibility belongs to God alone, who is the first and essential truth and who is never able to deceive or be deceived. All other infallibility, as communicated for a specific purpose, has its limits and its conditions under which it is considered to be present. The same is valid in reference to the infallibility of the Roman Pontiff. For this infallibility is bound by certain limits and conditions. What those conditions may be should be deduced not *a priori* but from the very promise or manifestation of the will of Christ. Now what follows from the promise of Christ, made to Peter and his successors, as far as these conditions are concerned? He promised Peter the gift of inerrancy in Peter's relation to the Universal Church: "You are Peter, and on this rock I will build my Church, and the gates of hell shall not prevail against it..." (Mt. 16:18). "Feed my lambs, feed my sheep" (Jn. 21:13-17). Peter, placed outside this relation to the universal Church, does not enjoy in his successors this charism of truth which comes from that certain promise of Christ. Therefore, in reality, the infallibility of the Roman Pontiff is restricted by reason *of the subject,* that is when the Pope, constituted in the chair of Peter, the center of the Church, speaks as universal teacher and supreme judge: it is restricted by reason of the *object,* i.e., when treating of matters of faith and morals; and by reason

---

The Synod of Pistoia, held in Italy in 1786, issued many decrees of a semi-Jansenist and Gallican flavor. The first of its 85 decrees condemned by Pius VI in 1794 reads: "In these latter times there has been spread a general obscuring of the more important truths concerning religion, etc." The statement is condemned as heretical, and Gasser avails himself of this opportunity to recall the condemnation (DS. 2601) and to indicate how papal infallibility helps make such a situation impossible.

of the *act* itself, i.e., when the Pope defines what must be believed or rejected by all the faithful.

Nevertheless, some of the most reverend fathers, not content with these conditions, go farther and even want to put into this constitution conditions which are found in different ways in different theological treatises and which concern the good faith and diligence of the Pontiff in searching out and enunciating the truth. However, these things, since they concern the conscience of the Pontiff rather than his relation [to the Church], must be considered as touching on the moral order rather than the dogmatic order. For with great care our Lord Jesus Christ willed that the charism of truth depend not on the conscience of the Pontiff, which is private—even most private—to each person, and known to God alone, but rather on the public relation of the Pontiff to the universal Church. If it were otherwise, this gift of infallibility would not be an effective means for preserving and repairing the unity of the Church. But in no way, therefore, should it be feared that the universal Church could be led into error about faith through the bad faith and negligence of the Pontiff. For the protection of Christ and the divine assistance promised to the successors of Peter is a cause so efficacious that the judgment of the supreme Pontiff would be impeded if it were to be erroneous and destructive of the

---

As he began his treatment of the three words "personal," "separate," and "absolute," Gasser stated that he was attempting to establish the "state of the question." In effect he has done this by using his commentary on the three words to set forth the limits of papal infallibility. He continues his exposition by noting that, in no way, is papal infallibility "absolute" since absolute infallibility belongs to God alone. Indeed, papal infallibility is limited by reason of its subject, object, and by the nature of the act itself. He will return to these limitations later in greater detail when he sets forth the explanation of the new formula of definition. In the meantime, he rejects argumentations which want conditions or limitations on papal infallibility written into the Draft itself.

Church; or, if in fact the Pontiff really arrives at a definition, it will truly stand infallibly.

But some will persist and say: there remains, therefore, the duty of the Pontiff—indeed most grave in its kind—of adhering to the means apt for discerning the truth, and, although this matter is not strictly dogmatic, it is, nevertheless, intimately connected with dogma. For we define: the [1215] dogmatic judgments of the Roman Pontiff are infallible. Therefore let us also define the form to be used by the Pontiff in such a judgment. It seems to me that this was the mind of some of the most reverend fathers as they spoke from this podium. But, most eminent and reverend fathers, this proposal simply cannot be accepted because we are not dealing with something new here. Already thousands and thousands of dogmatic judgments have gone forth from the Apostolic See; where is the law which prescribed the form to be observed in such judgments?

Perhaps someone will say: if we don't have a law, let us make one. But let us not do this lest we run up against that already condemned law which said that the council was above the Pope. Furthermore, of what use would be such a law? Would it not be completely useless, since it would never be able to be verified by the faithful and the bishops scattered throughout the world? Even more, it would be a very dangerous thing since it would offer the opportunity for innumerable foolish objections and anxieties. Therefore, let Peter gird himself according to the word of our Lord Jesus Christ, since Peter does not grow old while the world grows old but rather renews his powers like the eagle.

But someone may still persist and say: but what about the human means, the aid of the Church, the assent of the Church, say, that is, that the witness and advice of the bishops is not only unable to be excluded from the definition of infallibility but should be put in the definition as being among the conditions which are a matter of faith. Therefore this condition is said to be a matter of faith, and just how is that assertion proved? Is it contained in the promise of Christ? It seems to me that not only is it not contained in that promise, but rather that in that promise the contrary is contained. Indeed it cannot be denied that, in the relation of Peter to the Church, to which Christ willed that the infallibility of Peter be joined, there is contained a special relation of Peter to the Apostles and therefore also to the bishops, since Christ said to Peter: "I have prayed for you, that your faith may not fail, and you, once turned, confirm your brothers" (Lk. 22:32). This, therefore, is the relation of the Pontiff to the bishops which is contained in the promise of Christ. If these words of Christ are to have their necessary force, then it seems to me that one should conclude that the brothers, that is, the bishops, in order that they be firm in the faith, need the aid and advice of Peter and his successors, and not vice versa. Thus it happens that those who favor this opinion do not call upon Sacred Scripture but upon certain axioms which to them seem completely conclusive. What are these axioms?

First axiom: the members should be joined to the head and the head to the members. From this axiom they deduce that it is necessary for the Pope, in defining dogmas of faith, to do nothing without the advice and consent of his brothers. Before I reply to this objection, it will be helpful to remember that, in this opinion of the adversaries, we are dealing with a strict and absolute necessity of episcopal advice and help in every dogmatic judgment of the Roman Pontiff, so much so that it must have its place in the very definition of our dogmatic constitution. It is in this strict and absolute necessity that the whole difference between us consists. The difference does not consist in the opportuneness or some relative necessity which must be completely left to the judgment of the Roman Pontiff as he determines according to the circumstances. As such, this type of necessity cannot have a place in the definition of a dogmatic constitution.

That said, I return to the axiom about head and members and make my response. A figure of speech is not an argument, or, as is commonly said, every analogy limps. And that this comparison, applied in this way, really limps, can be [1216] shown by the following reason. Are not the laity, among whom there are very many who are outstanding in knowledge and piety, and, even more, are not the priests who exercise the duty of teaching their parishioners, are not they all members of the Church? Who would doubt it? Therefore, should these also help the Pope by their advice and aid when he makes dogmatic judgments? By no means. And why not? Is it not because they do not belong to the Church teaching? All right, but at the same time it is evident that the analogy about the head and members limps. But now it is asked whether the bishops also—although they are constituted by God as witnesses, teachers and judges of the Christian faith—do not relate to the Pope as disciples to teacher, when he is defining for the whole Church and exercising his duty as universal teacher. Such is the case. For this is what the words of Christ and the words "supreme judge," "universal doctor," and "pastor of the whole flock of Christ" signify. So, on that point, too, the adduced comparison limps, and the consequence about the necessity of the advice of the bishops falls.

I now push on to the end; we are almost there. But again there are some who insist and say: what you have said about a solemn definition of the Pope is true *post factum,* for then not only the laity but even priests and bishops are held to submit to the infallible authority of the Pope. But this is not true before the definition is made: in order to issue such a definition there should be the concurrence of the bishops. For (and this is the second axiom), just as the bishops are not able to do anything in determining dogmas without the Pope, so the Pope is not able to do anything without the bishops. Now let us look at this axiom from each side. The bishops are not able to do anything without the Pope in establishing dogmas of the Faith. This is true since even decrees about faith put forth by a general council are not infallible and firm unless they have been confirmed by the Pope.

The reason for this is not that which—I am sorry to say—has been several times indicated from this platform, namely the reason which says that all infallibility of the Church is situated in the Pope alone and from the Pope is derived and communicated to the Church. Indeed, according to a very celebrated theological system, this is able to be said about jurisdiction since the nature of jurisdiction is such that it is able to be, even should be, communicated to others. However, how is infallibility to be communicated? This I don't understand. The true reason why the bishops, even gathered in a general council, are not infallible in matters of faith and morals without the Pope is to be found in the fact that Christ promised this infallibility to the whole magisterium of the Church, that is, to the Apostles together with Peter. He did this when He said: "I am with you until the consummation of the world" (Mt. 28:20). Therefore the bishops are not able to do anything in this regard without the Pope. But is the other case true, viz., that the Pope is not able to do anything in this regard without the bishops? This other part has no value, since Christ said to Peter alone: "You are Peter (Mt. 16:18).... I have prayed for you that your faith may not fail (Lk. 22:32)."

But the issue is pressed by saying (and this is the third axiom): the consent of the Churches is a rule of faith which even the Pope ought to follow, and therefore he should consult those who rule the Churches before he makes a definition in order that he may be certain about the consent of the Churches. I reply. The matter has come to its extreme point and we must accurately distinguish between true and false lest we suffer shipwreck in port. It is true that the Pope in his definitions *ex cathedra* has the same sources *(fontes)* which the Church has, viz., Scripture and tradition. It is true that the consent of the present preaching of the whole magisterium of the Church, united with its head, is a rule of faith even for pontifical definitions. But from all that it can in no way be deduced that there is a strict and absolute necessity of seeking that consent from the rulers of the Churches or from the bishops. I say this because this consent is very frequently able to be deduced from the clear and manifest testimonies of [1217] Sacred Scripture, from the consent of antiquity, that is, of the Holy Fathers, from the opinion of theologians and from other private means, all of which suffice for full information about the fact of the Church's consent.

Finally it must never be overlooked that there is present to the Pope the Tradition of the Church of Rome, that is, of that Church to which faithlessness has no access and with which, because of its more powerful primacy, every Church must agree. Therefore that strict necessity [i.e., of consulting the bishops], such as is required for a dogmatic constitution, can in no way be demonstrated. It can happen that there be so difficult a case that the Pope thinks it necessary, for his own information, to ask the bishops, as an ordinary means, what the sense of the Churches is, as he did, for example, in the case of the Immaculate Conception. Such a case, however, is not able to be established as a rule.

Furthermore—and this is to be noted well—everyone knows that this rule about the consent of the Churches in their present preaching is valid only in its positive sense and, by no means, in its negative sense. This means that everything which the Universal Church, consenting to, receives and venerates in its present preaching as revealed is certainly true and Catholic [doctrine]. But, what happens if disagreements arise among the particular churches and are followed by controversies about the faith? Then, according to Vincent of Lerins, one must recur to the consent of antiquity, that is, to Scripture and the holy Fathers; and, from the consent of antiquity, differences in present preaching are to be resolved.

Likewise it is to be noted that dogmatic judgments of the Roman Pontiff are especially concerned with controversies about the faith in which recourse has been had to the Holy See; and the Pontiff should therefore define them, either from the Scriptures, the holy Fathers, or Doctors of the Church, or from the Tradition of the Church of Rome which faithfully and religiously has preserved what Peter passed down. Therefore whoever contends that the Pope, either for his information or for an infallible judgment about faith and morals, totally depends on the manifest consent of the bishops or on their aid has nothing left to do than to establish that false principle which says that all dogmatic judgments of the Roman Pontiff are weak and reformable in and of themselves unless the consent of the Church accrues to them. But such an outlook is either completely arbitrary or subversive of all papal infallibility. It is arbitrary if it requires the assent of a greater or lesser part of the bishops. Because, who will decide what number of them is sufficient? Who will make a choice since, in this respect, the bishops are completely equal among themselves and the assent of some cannot be prejudicial to the assent and judgment of others? The arbitrary character of this outlook is seen especially when one is dealing with subsequent assent, either tacit or expressed. History is a witness to what anxieties, commotions and scandals come forth. But, wait, there is more. This system or outlook is completely subversive of all papal infallibility if the consent of the whole Church is required by it. For then there would exist in reality only one infallibility, that which resides in the whole body of the teaching Church. But in that case, the decrees of the Roman Pontiff can and should be

---

In his argumentation against all efforts to insert conditions for the exercise of papal infallibility into the definition itself, Gasser makes several significant points. 1) The obligation to use all suitable means for ascertaining the truth is a moral duty incumbent on the Pope, and, as such, not the proper object of a dogmatic definition. The gift of inerrancy in defining a doctrine of faith or morals is given to the Pope as a public person in the Church and is given for the sake of the preservation of truth in the Church. Even if bad faith or negligence were to be present in a Pope's efforts to ascertain the truth, divine Providence, while holding him accountable, would see to it that a solemn definition would not happen or would be, in fact, inerrant despite the moral lapse of the Pontiff. 2) In his efforts to ascertain the truth, the Pope can only draw on the same sources (fonts) which are the property of the entire Church, viz., Scripture and Tradition, but, in this regard, he has the powerful aid of the Tradition of the Roman Church whose inerrant instinct for the faith history has demonstrated. 3) The *sensus Ecclesiae* is an essential source for ascertaining the truth, and, in cases of current dispute as to what

reformed by a general council inasmuch as, in the meantime, the assent of the Church would not be so manifest that it could not be denied. And lest we fall again into the infallibility of the Pontiff decreeing by himself alone, the Pope would not be able to confirm any but those decrees of a council which were pleasing to a majority of the bishops or rather to the unanimity of the bishops. But what if the bishops did not agree among themselves? It would be the end of judgment in the Church, it would be the death knell of the Church which, according to the Apostle, should be the column and foundation of truth. Now before I end this general relatio, I should [1218] respond to the most grave objection which has been made from this podium, viz. that we wish to make the extreme opinion of a certain school of theology a dogma of Catholic faith. Indeed this is a very grave objection, and, when I heard it from the mouth of an outstanding and most esteemed speaker, I hung my head sadly and pondered well before speaking. Good God, have you so confused our minds and our tongues that we are misrepresented as promoting the elevation of the extreme opinion of a certain school to the dignity of dogma, and is Bellarmine brought forth as the author

---

the *sensus Ecclesiae* is, one must have recourse to what was held on the matter in times previous to the current controversy. 4) The notion that infallibility resides in the Pope alone and is communicated to the Church in the same way that some theologians hold to be true of jurisdiction is a notion to be rejected. 5) Setting as a condition the antecedent or consequent consent of the bishops is something which has no historical precedent and one which would involve endless disputes concerning what number of the bishops would have to consent and what form their consent would have to take. Such an approach Gasser calls "arbitrary or subversive" and attempts to show its difficulties by a *reductio ad absurdum* argument.

Before completing his general relatio and turning to the suggested corrections to the Draft, Gasser considers one last charge of those opposed to the Draft, viz., that it is simply "canonizing" the most extreme pro-papal opinions of one school of theology, that of Albert Pighius.

of the fourth proposition of the Declaration of the French Clergy? For, if I may begin from the last point, what is the difference between the assertion which the reverend speaker attributes to Bellarmine, viz., "The Pontiff is not able to define anything infallibly without the other bishops and without the cooperation of the Church," and that well-known 4th article which says: "in questions of faith the judgment of the supreme Pontiff is not irreformable unless the consent of the Church accrues to it"? In reality there is hardly to be found any difference unless someone wants to call the disagreement of the bishops the cooperation of the Church so that a dogmatic definition would be infallible, even though the bishops dissent, but as long as they had been consulted beforehand. These things are said about the opinion of Bellarmine. As far as the doctrine set forth in the Draft goes, the Deputation is unjustly accused of wanting to raise an extreme opinion, viz., that of Albert Pighius, to the dignity of a dogma. For the opinion of Albert Pighius, which Bellarmine indeed calls pious and probable, was that the Pope, as an individual person or a private teacher, was able to err from a type of ignorance but was never able to fall into heresy or teach heresy. To say nothing of the other points, let me say that this is clear from the very words of Bellarmine, both in the citation made by the reverend speaker and also from Bellarmine himself who, in book 4, chapter VI, pronounces on the opinion of Pighius in the following words: "It can be believed probably and piously that the supreme Pontiff is not

Albert Pighius (Pigge) was a Dutch theologian (c. 1490-1542) and a strong defender of papal infallibility in a sometimes exaggerated form. He is generally understood to have defended the thesis that the Pope, even as a private person, was incapable of falling into heresy. Using Robert Bellarmine as a source, Gasser maintains that this is a probable and pious opinion, but, it is not this opinion that the Draft proposes to define since Gasser has been at pains to stress that the Draft is treating the Pope in his role as public person, supreme teacher of the Church, when he defines doctrine of faith or morals for the entire Church, a position Bellarmine held as "common and certain."

only not able to err as Pontiff but that even as a particular person he is not able to be heretical, by pertinaciously believing something contrary to the faith." From this, it appears that the doctrine in the proposed chapter is not that of Albert Pighius or the extreme opinion of any school, but rather that it is one and the same which Bellarmine teaches in the place cited by the reverend speaker and which Bellarmine adduces in the fourth place and calls most certain and assured, or rather, correcting himself, the most common and certain opinion.

I will now set forth the first of the suggested corrections and then a vote will be able to be had on them, namely on numbers one to twenty inclusive. After the general relatio, the individual corrections will now be able to be dealt with briefly.

Having completed the general *relatio,* Gasser now turns to consider in turn each of the proposed corrections to the Draft. Speaking on behalf of the Deputation *de fide,* he will accept some of the suggestions and reject others. It should be noted, however, that acceptance or rejection by the Deputation is itself only a suggestion since all the proposed corrections—except those which have only expressed a wish for a certain change without formulating that wish in the form of an emendation, or those which are totally contrary to the purpose of the Draft which has already been accepted by the bishops as the "working document"—will be submitted to the general congregation, i.e., to the assembled body of bishops, for a vote.

The proposed corrections are considered in an order which follows the title and two paragraph format of the Draft. Gasser will note, however, that the Deputation itself has suggested an emendation to the Draft by means of an insertion between paragraphs one and two. This emendation he refers to as the "insertion" found in the folio distributed to the bishops on July 9 and is found on pp. 11-13 above.

The voting on the suggested corrections followed the completion of Gasser's *relatio,* and the results of that voting (found in *Mansi,* 52, 1231-1232) are indicated in the commentary on the various proposed corrections.

The first eight suggested corrections concern the title of the proposed chapter. The first four want the title to read: *On the supreme magisterium,* or simply, *On the magisterium,* or *On the primacy of magisterium.* But the Deputation was not able to approve such a title, because it would appear to be broader than the matter treated in this chapter. In this chapter we are not dealing in general with the supreme magisterium of the Pope, which is part of his jurisdiction, since the jurisdiction of the Pope has two facets, (lit. keys), that is, of knowledge and of power. Therefore the Deputation was not able to accept the first, the second (under its parts a, b, c), the third or the fourth suggested corrections.

Suggested correction #5 wants the title to read: *On the infallible magisterium of the Roman Pontiffs.* This correction the Deputation has accepted with one reservation, viz., that it not be of Roman Pontiffs in the plural, but in the singular, i.e., *On the infallible magisterium of the Roman Pontiff.* The reason for the admission of the suggested correction is this: the title *On the infallibility of the Roman Pontiff* when translated into other languages sometimes does not have its [1219] proper sense. For example, in German, this way of putting it is able to be confused with impeccability. Therefore, so that it may immediately be clear that we are not treating of the impeccability of the Roman Pontiff but of his infallibility in teaching, let the chapter be entitled *On the infallible magisterium of the Roman Pontiff.*

Suggested correction #5 was proposed by Konrad Martin (1812-1879), bishop of Paderborn from 1856 until his death. He had previously been a teacher of moral theology, and had studied under Dollinger, the German theologian who ultimately left the Church in reaction to the definition of papal infallibility. At Vatican I, Martin was a member of the Deputation *de fide* and a chief formulator of the final definition of faith on infallibility. His suggestion concerning the title of the Dogmatic Constitution, put into the singular as Gasser notes, was accepted in the subsequent voting (cf. *Mansi,* 52, 1231). Suggestions #6, 7, and 8 were rejected in the subsequent voting (cf. *Idem).*

Suggested correction #6 is not admitted because it places a reason in the title, citing the Pope as head of the teaching Church. But in a title there should not be anything about reasons.

Suggested correction #7 is also not admissible. According to the mind of the one who suggested it, the title should read: *On the infallibility of the Roman Pontiff in exercising the office of the supreme magisterium,* thus immediately circumscribing the infallibility of the Pontiff in a certain way. But it is not customary to place in the titles the limits of what is to be subsequently treated.

Finally, suggested correction #8 is not a title, but rather a whole thesis and therefore is also not able to be accepted.

Suggested correction #9. No vote will be asked on this suggested correction because it only contains a kind of wish that the documents of the councils be omitted and that the divine promise [only] be adduced as an argument for infallibility.

Suggested correction #10 begins the proposals which touch upon the first part of the proposed chapter, i.e., on the introduction which is contained in the opening words, and on the documents of the three councils. Indeed, suggested corrections #10, #11, and #12 propose a new text for the first part of this proposed chapter. Suggested correction #10 consists of three parts. The Deputation accepts the first part because the style is more elegant while the sense is identical with the proposed chapter.

The second part of proposed correction #10, beginning with the words "With the approbation of the Council of Lyons" up to the words "The Council of Florence defined in solemn decree" will not be submitted to vote, but it is also not accepted because it has already been decided that not only would the Council of Lyons be adduced [as evidence], but that these documents of the three Councils should remain completely intact. Only certain things which are found in the folio distributed yesterday under the numbers 1-5 should be emended as far as style and a more correct text are concerned, and this because of the fact that the Deputation proposed that, after the first paragraph which contains the documents of the Councils, there should be inserted a description of the *praxis* of the Apostolic See in respect to dogmatic judgments. Since that part is historical, as is the first part, which treats of the documents, it should be proposed in an historical form and not in the form of a solemn profession of faith as it is now found in the proposed chapter where one reads "we profess with the council, etc." But since this matter also touches on style, it too will not be submitted to a vote.

As far as a more correct text is concerned, especially worthy of note is the correction under #3 of the folio distributed yesterday. The learned and reverend bishop of Rottenburg also suggested that the words as found in the present Draft do not completely agree with the correct text of the 4th Council of Constantinople. Therefore, the third correction is proposed according to this more correct text but is also not submitted to a vote.

The third part of this suggested correction #10 begins with the words, "In order that they might satisfy this pastoral obligation." In place of this third part as it is found in correction #10 itself, we put forth for the vote of the fathers the [1220] correction which was printed up and distributed to everyone yesterday. This correction is strongly recommended in order to satisfy both those who think that the cooperation of the

---

Bishop Martin of Paderborn is also the author of suggested correction #10. Of the three parts of this suggestion, parts one and three were accepted by the bishops in the subsequent voting, following the recommendation of Gasser. Part two was not submitted for a vote. By comparing the Draft with the insertion proposed by the Deputation on July 9, and the final form of Chapter IV of *Pastor Aeternus,* one can see that the influence of Martin, through suggested correction #10, was considerable.

The bishop of Rottenburg referred to by Gasser is Carl Josef von Hefele (1809-1893), noted Church historian and patrologist. He was a staunch opponent of the definition of infallibility, voted against the entire chapter on July 13 and left Rome before the public vote on July 18.

Church is altogether excluded and those, who in their reflections and warnings, wanted to propose to the people different ways to illustrate this doctrine. Therefore, in this correction, newly adopted by the Deputation, beginning with the words "To satisfy this pastoral office..." and ending with the words "supreme apostolic office," in this newly adopted correction, I say, the following things are contained.

First there is described the care which the Roman Pontiffs have themselves undertaken in order to preserve and extend Catholic truth and which has been imposed on them by controversies over the faith which have arisen in various places and times. Then, beginning with the words, "Moreover the Roman Pontiffs, according to the dictates of times and circumstances..." there is described the procedure which the Roman Pontiffs have always used and use and will use in the future in respect to dogmatic definitions. Then, from the words, "to be consonant with Sacred Scripture and apostolic traditions..." there is described that that which the Roman Pontiffs define rests on Sacred Scripture and Tradition, under the protection of Christ and the assistance of the Holy Spirit, which protection and assistance is not to be confused with revelation. Then, beginning with the words, "All the venerable Fathers and holy orthodox doctors..." there is described the manner by which the definitions of the Roman Pontiff have been received, according to the promise of Christ, as conformed to truth and unchangeable, and how, by this very fact, the consent of the Churches dispersed throughout the world with the Roman Church and the Roman Church with them shines forth. Then, from the words, "Therefore this charism of truth..." there is described the purpose for which Christ the Lord gave this prerogative of inerrancy to the Apostolic See or to the Roman Pontiff. For the purpose of this gift is the good of the Church so that she might fulfill her task for the salvation of all, namely the realization of correct doctrine, the unity of faith and charity and the undivided connection between the foundation and edifice of the Church. Finally, in the last insertion "Since in our times which especially..." there is first indicated the reason for this solemn definition of pontifical infallibility, and then the nature of this prerogative, viz. that it does not belong to the Pope as a private person but as exercising his office as supreme pastor. Therefore this correction is recommended to the reverend fathers as suitable for acceptance.

Suggested correction #11. This suggested correction also contains a new text for the first part, i.e., for the first paragraph of our Draft. The ideas which occur in this suggestion are good enough but nevertheless the Deputation thinks this suggestion should not be accepted, especially because it does not seem that the public documents of the three ecumenical councils should be omitted.

Suggested correction #12. This suggestion also has an entirely new text for the first paragraph of our Draft, and the ideas in the suggestion are likewise very beautiful. But they are also, it seems to me, somewhat exaggerated. For this reason, and for the same reason which I cited in the previous suggestion, the Deputation thinks that this suggestion should not be accepted.

Suggested corrections #13—20 contain certain suggested corrections of individual parts of the first paragraph of our proposed chapter. In suggestion #13 there is expressed the wish that the seven first lines of our chapter, i.e., the introduction, be replaced by other words, viz., "That the Roman Pontiff as successor of St. Peter, Prince of the Apostles, etc." But it seems that this suggestion should not be accepted because the reason which the reverend author gives [1221] for his suggestion, i.e., that our manner of arguing proves the question by the question, which is to say that we demonstrate infallibility arguing from the primacy, does not in fact exist. The fact is that from the primacy we deduce the

Suggestion #12 was proposed by Bishop Caixal y Estrade of Urgal, Spain. He proposed that the object of infallibility was "every doctrine of faith and truth proposed by the Pope for the worship of God and salvation of souls" (cf. *Mansi*, 52, 1124). Gasser will return to the object of infallibility later.

supreme power of teaching, as one would deduce a species from its genus. From the supreme power of teaching, paying attention to its purpose, namely the preservation of unity in faith, and to the promises of Christ, we deduce infallibility. Therefore in reality there is not present that form of argumentation called the "vicious circle."

Suggestion #14 also pertains to the first words of the introduction of our chapter, desiring that they read as follows: "With the divine words shedding their light...and as the holy witness of the Liturgy testifies." But these words, particularly the final ones, can hardly be inserted in our chapter, as fine as they may be, since in fact, in our chapter, there is nothing found in the whole teaching which is drawn from the liturgical documents.

Suggestion #15 wants to insert after the words "supreme power of teaching" a citation from St. Augustine which reads: "In the words of the Apostolic See the Catholic faith is so ancient, well-founded, certain and clear that it would be criminal for a Christian to doubt them." But, since these words of St. Augustine are not general but are made in reference to an individual case, they do not seem suitable for insertion in our chapter.

Suggestion #16. The reverend father desires that pontifical infallibility be deduced expressly from the apostolicity and indefectability of the Church. But in reality the apostolicity and indefectability of the Church are suggested in our chapter, and, anyway, not all the arguments can be or should be brought forth lest, if one be omitted, it seem to be of no importance. Therefore this suggestion is not proposed as being acceptable.

Suggestion #17 concerns style and therefore is not proposed for a vote.

Suggestion #18 consists of two parts. In the first part the author wills that the words of the Council of Florence either be quoted in their entirety or blotted out or only alluded to. But the words of Florence, it would appear, should not be taken away nor cited in their entirety insofar as they do not pertain to the infallible magisterium of the Pontiff. Therefore the first part of this suggestion should not be accepted. Likewise for the second part of the suggestion. For it is asserted in the second part that the Pontiff is only the guardian and teacher of the faith and not an infallible judge. Thus it is not suitable that this suggestion be proposed for acceptance by the fathers.

Suggestion #19. The reverend father wants the word "ecumenical" to be added to the reference to the Council of Florence. But this is surely unnecessary. Right from the beginning, when these documents are introduced, it is said that only those testimonies are brought forth which come from ecumenical councils. Therefore, since from the very beginning all three of these councils are called ecumenical, that is what is being affirmed of the Council of Florence.

Suggestion #20 is not proposed for a vote. It wishes to add the following after the words from the Council of Florence: "Moreover this fullness of power, according to the mind of the same Council, includes the infallible magisterium of the Roman Pontiff." But this suggestion has been fully provided for by correction #2 which is proposed for insertion between para. 1 and para. 2 of our chapter, or by the correction which is found in the folio distributed yesterday.

Suggestion #21 is not submitted for a vote because it contains a censure rather than a suggested correction. The reverend father wants that nothing be defined as of faith in the matter of infallibility.

Suggestion #22. A vote will also not be asked for this suggestion because the desires of the reverend father have been abundantly provided for in the paragraph which treats

---

Gasser's references to the "folio distributed yesterday" are to the insertions proposed on July 9 and found on pp. 11-13.

In the subsequent voting, suggested corrections #11-19 were denied approval by the bishops, thus following Gasser's recommendations, the recommendations, that is, of the Deputation *de fide*. Likewise, proposed corrections #20-29 were all dealt with or voted upon according to the recommendations made by the Deputation through Gasser.

of the praxis of the Apostolic See in matters of dogmatic judgments and which has been inserted between the first and second paragraphs.

Suggestion #23. The reverend father wants that, in the [1222] proposed chapter, there first be recorded the words of Christ, "Going teach all nations, etc." and then the three well-known citations of Sacred Scripture in favor of the infallibility of the Roman Pontiff. Inasmuch as the second part of this request would seem to have been abundantly provided for in those things which are found in the documents of the three Councils and in the paragraph which has been newly inserted, this suggestion is not proposed for acceptance.

Suggestion #24. No vote will be asked for this suggestion either, because it contains something which does not seem to pertain to a dogmatic constitution but rather to the mode of acting of the supreme Pontiff in promulgating decrees of the faith.

Suggestion #25. This suggestion is also not able to be accepted by the Deputation because it seems that the author of this suggestion wants to restrict pontifical infallibility to one of confirming decrees of general councils. There is therefore a total change, i.e., a passage from one thing to another.

Suggestion #26. This suggestion has been provided for both in the documents which are already in the proposed chapter, as well as in the paragraph newly inserted. Therefore there will be no vote asked.

Suggestion #27. The reverend father wants that the words of Christ, "I have prayed for you, etc.," (Lk. 22:32) be authentically declared by the Council. But an authentic declaration of this kind cannot be attempted and, if it were

---

Suggested correction #24 was put forth by Bishop Moriarty of Kerry, Ireland, requesting that no papal dogmatic definition be recognized as infallible unless it was accompanied by the "usual formula," viz., the Pope, "adhering to the vote of the cardinals of the Roman Church and of other teachers in sacred theology, etc."

attempted, there would surely be disagreement in the council about this matter. Therefore this suggestion is not proposed for acceptance.

Suggestion #28. This consists of two parts which indeed are not suitable for voting since they contain only the wish of the reverend father. Also, in my judgment the second of the two parts contains an opinion which cannot be allowed. It supposed that there is no other infallibility in the Church than that which is communicated to the Church through the Pontiff, as is the case with jurisdiction.

Suggestion #29. The reverend father wishes that there be added to the Roman Pontiff the words, "existing at the time." But, since this seems to be *per se* superfluous, it will not be submitted to a vote.

Suggestion #30. As far as the first part of the suggestion goes, the reverend father wants that the words "universal pastor" be substituted for the words "universal teacher." This desire is already satisfied in the new formula of the definition, about which I shall speak soon. As far as the second part of the suggestion is concerned, since very many fathers have requested that the well-known formula "speaking *ex cathedra*" be retained and since very many schools [of theology] have indeed used this solemn term in theology, the Deputation *de fide* thinks this desire should be satisfied, and therefore the second part of this suggestion is proposed for acceptance.

Suggestion #31. This contains the same request as the previous suggestion, except that in this case cogent reasons are given for the retention of the expression "the Pontiff speaking *ex cathedra*." No further vote is necessary, however, since this will be satisfied by accepting suggestion #30.

Suggestion #30 was proposed by Bishop Gandolfi of Corneto (Tarquinia), desiring that the words *ex cathedra* be inserted into the Draft before the words "he defines." As Gasser suggested, the proposal was accepted by the bishops in the voting (cf. *Mansi,* 52, 1231).

Suggestion #32. The request of this reverend father has already been satisfied in the paragraph recently inserted.

Suggestion #33. Now we come to the definition itself. The first suggestions concern certain preliminary matters, but the latter suggestions concern the formula of the definition itself. In suggestion #33, the reverend father appears to want that, having suppressed the reality and the word infallibility, the right and duty of the Roman Pontiff be defended as only that of proscribing heresies, ancient errors against the faith, and, should a new heresy arise, the right and duty of prescribing under pain of excommunication what must be held [1223] or rejected. As a result the Deputation is not able to permit this suggestion.

Suggestion #34. This suggestion is also not able to be allowed because it seems to exclude completely or, at least, restrict excessively the papal infallibility, properly so called. According to the mind of the reverend father who made the suggestion, the process in matters of our faith is as follows: the Roman Pontiff makes known the mind of the Church; the Church makes known the meaning of the deposit of revelation; revelation makes known the mind of God, whose truthfulness is the formal motive for faith. Therefore, to define the meaning of a revealed dogma seems to be, according to the mind of the reverend father, something which pertains only and exclusively to a general council or to the Church Universal.

Suggestion #35. The reverend father wants that the doctrine of infallibility be proposed by the council as being "true and Catholic doctrine," but not as being a truth *de fide*. In this way, he says, a leap [in theological development] will be avoided. But in fact our definition does not occur via any

---

Suggested correction #33 was proposed by Bishop Verot of St. Augustine, Florida, U.S.A., a firm opponent of the definition of papal infallibility.

Suggested corrections #33-35 were, as Gasser recommended, all voted down by the bishops (cf. *Mansi*, 52, 1231).

leap, since no part of Catholic doctrine has been so often and so vigorously aired, at least since the end of the seventeenth century, as has this part of our teaching. Therefore this council is certainly not able to be accused of having acted via any leap.

Suggestion #36. With this suggestion we begin the individual conditions which some of the reverend fathers want to be appended to the definition itself as conditions without which the infallibility of the Roman Pontiff cannot stand secure. According to the principles which I have already set forth in the general relatio, the Deputation is not able to admit any of these suggestions, which, nonetheless, should be submitted to the vote of the fathers for the sake of the liberty of the Council. The Deputation *de fide,* according to the principles I have set down, should and does exclude the following suggestions. What is more, those suggestions should all the more be excluded which are frequently very indefinite, so much so that, for that reason, they are more able to give

---

Suggested corrections #36 through #53 are mainly concerned with emending the Draft in such a way that certain conditions be placed on the manner of exercising papal infallibility. On behalf of the Deputation, Gasser rejects all such proposals. The "formula Antoniniana" is that based on the writings of Saint Antoninus (1389-1459), a Dominican and bishop of Florence. Suggested correction #39, put forth by Bishop von Ketteler of Mainz (who, along with Cardinal Manning of Westminster, was one of the outstanding leaders of the Catholic social movement in the nineteenth century, although the two were on opposite sides of the infallibility question at the Council) and suggested correction #40, put forth by Cardinal Rauscher of Vienna, both suggested the formula of St. Antoninus, although in slightly different forms. Von Ketteler asked that the words "using the advice of the bishops and the aid of the Church" be inserted into the Draft; Rauscher wanted the same insertion phrased as "The successor of St. Peter, using the advice and requiring the aid of the Church Universal, is not able to err, etc." (cf. *Mansi,* 52, 1128-1129).

Gasser, speaking for the Deputation, has, as seen above, admitted the moral obligation which the Pope has of seeking

opportunity for disputes than to be verified in reality. This is true even for that condition which is found in the so-called *formula Antoniniana*. For this formula would be too vague and indefinite for a conciliar definition (I am not speaking of a theological treatise). Therefore, the Deputation, for its part, simply rejects suggestion #36, although, nevertheless, it will, as I have said, be submitted to a vote. This suggestion consists of two parts. As far as the first part goes, the Deputation *de fide* replied negatively; as far as the second part is concerned, no vote will be taken because it does not pertain to a dogmatic constitution since it wants that the council, through an amendment to the dogmatic constitution, seek from the Holy Father the mode of agreement or cooperation of the bishops which must be observed in individual cases for a definition. Thus the Deputation also rejects suggestions #37, #38, #39 and #40. Suggestion #41 will not be submitted to a vote because it does not have a suggestion expressed in suitable words. Suggestion #42 is likewise excluded for the reason just given. Likewise is suggestion #43 rejected by the Deputation.

The first part of Suggestion #44 will not be submitted for a vote because it doesn't have words suitably composed for a correction. The second part contains conditions very vague and uncertain and thus this suggestion must also be rejected by the Deputation.

---

suitable advice, etc., before formulating a dogmatic definition. However, the Deputation was steadfast in refusing to set any conditions into the Draft itself, stating that the moral obligation was 1) ultimately for the Pope's conscience before God, 2) unsuitable for a dogmatic constitution, 3) open to ambiguous interpretations, 4) capable of being understood as a juridical limitation on the free exercise of the papal prerogative of infallibility, or even 5) a latent form of Gallicanism or conciliarism. In its refusal to admit any such condition, the Deputation was supported by the majority of the bishops, and no condition appears in the final dogmatic constitution. The bishops followed Gasser's recommendations in the voting on suggested corrections #36-44 (cf. *Mansi,* 52, 1231).

Suggestion #45 is also rejected. It has two parts. The first part seems to contain a certain condition, viz., "After a study prescribed by law, he brings forth [a decision] from the faith of the teaching Church." This suggestion or proposed [1224] correction is also very vague and ambiguous and thus is not able to be accepted. In the second part of this suggestion the reverend father wishes that the words "matters of faith and morals" be replaced by "the principles of faith and morals." But the Deputation *de fide* also cannot permit this suggestion, partly because this expression would be completely new

---

Suggestion #45 was put forth by Bishop Colet of Lucon, France. The first part of the suggested correction is, like the previous ones, a certain condition on the exercise of papal infallibility. The second part requested a change in the wording of the definition so that it would read: "...by his apostolic authority, he defines what must be *believed* by the Universal Church as of faith in matters of faith and the *principles of morals*" (cf. *Mansi*, 52, 1130).

The second part of Colet's suggested correction is actually out of place here. It concerns the *object* of infallibility, or, more precisely, the matters which the Pope is able to define infallibly. Furthermore, the suggested correction is not Colet's own. When he proposed it, he explicitly stated (cf. *Mansi*, 52, 983-986, at the end) that he was merely repeating and agreeing with the suggested correction of Bishop Yusto of Burgos, Spain. In the order in which Gasser has lined up the suggestions, however, Bishop Yusto's proposal is treated as suggested correction #58. Since Colet's proposal cannot be properly understood apart from Yusto's and since both are better seen once Gasser has completed his comments on the *object of infallibility*, comment on both of them will be found at that point in the text. Sufficient to note here is that the Deputation found the suggestion unacceptable and that the bishops subsequently voted against it (cf. *Mansi*, 52, 1231). One comment will suffice here. Gasser remarks that the words "matters of faith and morals" should be retained because "every theologian knows what is to be understood by these words." What was at issue was not "matters of faith" but rather "matters of morals" since the suggestion had been to replace

whereas the expression "matter of faith and morals," i.e., doctrine of faith and morals, is very well known and every theologian knows what is to be understood by these words. Furthermore the principles of morals are able to be other merely philosophical principles of natural moral goodness *(naturalis honestatis)*, which do not pertain to the deposit of faith in every respect.

"matters of morals" with "principles of morals." Now what was understood by "matters of morals"? It was a very wide understanding indeed. "Matters of morals" included not only what was directly revealed by God, but also the natural law, and the specific, concrete decisions which the Church had to make on moral matters for which an answer was not found in revelation. That the matters of morals were interpreted thus broadly can be seen by looking at two of the major theologians present at the Council itself. The Jesuit John Baptist Franzelin (1816-1886) held that the natural law was included under "matters of morals" (cf. his *Tractatus De Divina Traditione et Scriptura*, 4th ed., Rome, 1896, p. 112, *"...tuum leges practicae [et in his etiam lex naturalis scripta in cordibus hominum ratione utentium]...."*) He actually held that these things pertain to the "deposit of faith." Another Jesuit, Joseph Kleutgen (1811-1883), a philosopher and theologian, went to Vatican I as the theologian for Konrad Martin of Paderborn, and was the official presentor to the Deputation *de fide* of the draft chapter on the proposed dogmatic constitution on the Church. In his remarks at that time, Kleutgen set forth the position which holds that "matters of morals" include particular and specific moral decisions for which "an answer cannot be found in revelation itself" (cf. *Mansi*, 53, 327, #4; a translation will be found below in our treatment of suggested correction #58). Finally, it should be noted that Gasser passes over in silence Colet's suggestion which would replace the "what must be held" of the Draft with "what must be believed" (cf. Colet's original suggestion, *Mansi*, 52, 986). The reason for this, however, can be learned from Kleutgen's presentation on the dogmatic constitution on the Church before the Deputation *de fide* on July 14: the "to be believed" is too restrictive a terminology (cf. *Mansi*, 53, 326). We shall return to this later when speaking of the extension of infallibility.

Suggestion #46 will not be submitted for a vote because the intent of the reverend father seems to be sufficiently provided for in the paragraph recently inserted into the proposed chapter.

Suggestion #47 can also not be permitted, not because of proposed conditions [on infallibility] but for another reason. The reverend father appears to restrict pontifical infallibility only to controversies of faith, whereas the Pontiff is also infallible as universal teacher and as supreme witness of Tradition, the deposit of faith.

Suggestion #48. This suggestion, too, cannot be accepted, at least not according to the intention of the one who proposed it, since it says: "When the Pontiff defines, exercising his office as head of the Church which always teaches with him, etc." These words carry with them an ambiguous sense and because of that ambiguity the suggestion cannot be accepted.

Suggestion #49 is also such that it carries an ambiguous sense. It says: "By his apostolic authority, as head of the Church and always united by divine will with the body of bishops."

Suggestion #50. The reverend father wants that we say only "as head of the Church." This desire is equivalently fulfilled in those things which are found in the new formula of the definition, since all things said there about the Pope defining are to be equivalently taken as meaning "as head of the Church."

Suggestion #51. This suggestion also appears unsuitable for a vote. The reverend father wants that there be inserted the words, partly taken from Father Perrone (the mention of whom was omitted in the last insertion by an oversight) and partly from St. Augustine. But the first citation is not able to

---

Suggested corrections #46-53 are sufficiently clear as to need no comment. In the subsequent voting, the recommendations of the Deputation as expressed by Gasser were followed in each case.

be inserted because in reality no place is found for it. As far as the words of St. Augustine, viz., "that which the ancient Apostolic See and the Roman Church perseveringly holds along with the other churches," are concerned, they are found in the paragraph recently inserted. Therefore, although these words do not occur in exactly the same context, the intention of the reverend father seems to have been satisfied, and so no vote will be taken on this suggestion.

Suggestion #52 wants the following words: "When he defines *ex cathedra,* by his apostolic authority, what is contained in the deposit of tradition about matters of faith and morals, and therefore what must be held by all as a matter of faith or is to be rejected as contrary to faith, he is not able to err because of divine assistance; for he is the head of the Body of Christ, etc." Although all these words are able to have a correct meaning, they are, nevertheless, ambiguous. The mind of the reverend father seems to be that the Pope promulgates [doctrine] with the consent of the bishops or of the teaching Church. Therefore, according to the mind of the Deputation this suggestion should not be accepted.

Suggestion #53 will not be submitted to a vote because it only contains the proposal that no conditions be set forth in the definition of papal infallibility itself. So much for the conditions.

Suggestion #51 was made by Bishop Landriot of Rheims who wanted the Draft to indicate more clearly the union existing between the Pope and the Church, between the Church of Rome and the other Churches (cf. *Mansi,* 52, 840ff.). To do this he proposed using a formula taken from the *De locis theol.* (Ip. sect. 2, cap. IV) of Rev. Giovanni Perrone, S.J. Perrone (1794-1876) was a famous teacher of theology in Rome who had helped prepare the definition of the Immaculate Conception of Our Lady.

Having completed his comments on suggested corrections #1-53, and made recommendations on behalf of the Deputation in respect to how the bishops should treat the suggested corrections (all of which recommendations were followed in the subse-

[1225]   The rest of the suggestions concern the ambit or extension of papal infallibility, and at this point there will be set forth for a vote the new formula, recently adopted by the Deputation and found in the folio distributed yesterday. The formula, as you know, goes as follows: "Therefore, faithfully adhering to the tradition received from the beginning of the Christian religion, for the glory of God our Savior, for the exaltation of the Catholic faith and the salvation of the Christian people, and with the approval of the holy council, we teach and define that it is a divinely revealed doctrine that the Roman Pontiff, when he speaks *ex cathedra,* that is, when exercising his office as pastor and teacher of all Christians, by his supreme apostolic authority, [defines] a doctrine of faith—the definitions of the Roman Pontiff are irreformable of themselves."

This suggested correction is, in a way, in harmony with suggestion #68 which is, therefore, transferred to this place. It harmonizes with that suggestion, although not completely. After many discussions which were held in the Deputation *de fide* about this matter, the entire Deputation *de fide* finally

---

quent voting), Gasser turns now to the actual definition itself. In this case, he is no longer discussing the original Draft, but rather the reformulation of the part of that Draft which contained the definition. That reformulation is found on pp. 12-13 above. It is very like the suggested correction proposed by Cardinal Cullen of Dublin, Ireland (cf. *Mansi,* 52, 751-752, 1135) as Gasser notes when he brings forth Cullen's suggested correction #68 to be treated at this point. Gasser now gives a detailed explanation of the meaning of the proposed definition, treating the 1) subject of the definition, i.e., the Pope as public person, 2) the nature and condition of the infallible act itself, 3) the cause for the infallible nature of the act, i.e., the assistance of the Holy Spirit, and 4) the object of the act, i.e., the matters which are covered by the gift of infallibility, or the extension of the gift. The first point, viz., the subject of the definition, Gasser deals with summarily since he has spoken already on this when he dealt with "personal," "absolute," and "separate" in reference to papal infallibility.

agreed unanimously that this suggestion or rather this new formula for the definition of papal infallibility would be submitted to the general congregation. Since this matter is of such great importance, I will set forth here the meaning of this new formula of definition.

In this definition we treat 1) the subject of infallibility, namely the Roman Pontiff as Pontiff, i.e., as a public person in relation to the Universal Church.

2) There is contained in the definition the act, or the quality and condition of the act of an infallible pontifical definition, i.e., the Pontiff is said to be infallible when he speaks *ex cathedra*. This formula is received in the schools, and the meaning of this formula as it is found in the very body of the definition is as follows: when the supreme Pontiff speaks *ex cathedra*, not, first of all, when he decrees something as a private teacher, nor only as the bishop and ordinary of a particular See and province, but when he teaches as exercising his office as supreme pastor and teacher of all Christians. Sec-

---

It is here on point two that Gasser may be said to have stumbled for the only time in his presentation if one views the speech from the point of view of its effect on his audience. The majority of the bishops follow the recommendation of the Deputation as given by Gasser and accept the new formula, but, once approved, the bishops were allowed to present certain "exceptions" to individual parts of the formula. As can be seen from a study of these exceptions *(Mansi,* 52, 1276-1302) a number of the bishops thought that the word "defines" was too restrictive and too juridical. As a result, Gasser ascended the podium again on July 16 to give a final relatio to the general congregation in order to clarify what the Deputation *de fide* understood by the word "defines." His comments on the sixteenth were as follows:

"My second observation concerns the word 'define' as it is found in our Draft. It is obvious from the many exceptions that this word is an obstacle for some of the reverend fathers; hence, in their exceptions, they have completely eliminated this word or have substituted another word, viz., 'decree,' or something similar, in its place, or have said, simultaneously, 'defines and

ondly, not just any manner of proposing the doctrine is sufficient even when he is exercising his office as supreme pastor and teacher. Rather, there is required the manifest intention of defining doctrine, either of putting an end to a doubt about a certain doctrine or of defining a thing, giving a definitive judgment and proposing that doctrine as one which must be held by the Universal Church. This last point is indeed something intrinsic to every dogmatic definition of faith or morals which is taught by the supreme pastor and teacher of the Universal Church and which is to be held by the Universal Church. Indeed this very property and note of a definition, properly so-called, should be expressed, at least in some way, since he is defining doctrine to be held by the Universal Church. ·

3. There is found in the definition the principle or efficacious cause of infallibility. That principle or efficacious cause of infallibility is the protection of Christ and the assistance of the Holy Spirit.

---

decrees,' etc. Now I shall explain in a very few words how this word 'defines' is to be understood according to the Deputation *de fide*. Indeed, the Deputation *de fide* is not of the mind that this word should be understood in a juridical sense (Lat. *in sensu forensi*) so that it only signifies putting an end to controversy which has arisen in respect to heresy and doctrine which is properly speaking *de fide*. Rather, the word 'defines' signifies that the Pope directly and conclusively pronounces his sentence about a doctrine which concerns matters of faith or morals and does so in such a way that each one of the faithful can be certain of the mind of the Apostolic See, of the mind of the Roman Pontiff; in such a way, indeed, that he or she knows for certain that such and such a doctrine is held to be heretical, proximate to heresy, certain or erroneous, etc., by the Roman Pontiff. Such, therefore, is the meaning of the word 'defines.'

It can be said in truth that this final relatio adds nothing to what Gasser had already said on the subject in his major relatio of July 11th. Nonetheless, it does call attention to certain facts readily overlooked in the July 11th speech. The Pope, according to the Deputation, acts infallibly when, as pastor and teacher of

4. There is contained in the definition the object of infallibility. Infallibility has been promised in order to guard and unfold the integral deposit of faith. From this it can easily be seen that, in general, the object of infallibility is doctrine about faith and morals. But not all truths which pertain to the doctrine of faith and Christian morals are of the same kind. Nor are they all necessary in one and the same degree in order to guard the integrity of the faith. Therefore it follows that the errors which are opposed to guarding the deposit of faith are opposed in different degrees, just as the truths themselves, to which the errors are opposed, pertain to the same deposit in different degrees. These different degrees of error are distinguished by different notes of censure.

1. It is certain that the infallibility promised by God [1226] completely includes the same extent of truths whether that infallibility resides in the whole Church teaching, when it defines truths in council, or in the supreme Pontiff considered in himself. This is so since the purpose of infallibility is the same in whichever mode it is exercised.

---

the Universal Church, he definitively passes judgments—and intends to do so—on some matter of faith and morals. Furthermore, this characteristic, viz., of definitively passing judgment, must be "expressed, at least in some way" (relatio of July 11). Nevertheless, the Pope is not bound to any particular formula when he passes such a definitive judgment, nor is such an infallibly definitive judgment limited to matters which are, strictly speaking, *de fide,* since Gasser, speaking for the Deputation, expressly states that such a definitive act can touch upon the so-called "lesser censures" ("proximate to heresy," "certain or erroneous," etc.). In short, the word "defines" means, quite simply, "passing a definitive judgment" and doing so in such a way that it is recognized as being such. As far as the matters on which that type of a definitive judgment can be passed while still falling under the protection of the gift of infallibility—that is a question dealt with under point four of the July 11th relation (cf. p. 75 above).

2. In the very word of God by which infallibility, whether considered in the Pope *per se* or in the Church teaching, has been promised in order to guard the deposit of faith, there is undoubtedly contained the fact that this infallibility extends at least to those things which in themselves constitute the deposit of faith, namely, which are necessary for defining the dogmas of the faith and, what comes to the same thing, for condemning heresies. Hence it clearly is believed and must be believed as a matter of faith by all the children of holy Mother Church that the Church is infallible in proposing and defining dogmas of faith. Now in the same manner, the infallibility of the head of the Church is not able to be revealed and defined unless, by that very fact, it is revealed and defined that the Pontiff is infallible in defining dogmas of faith.

3. But, together with revealed truths, there are, as I said a little while ago, other truths more or less strictly connected. These truths, although they are not revealed *in se,* are nevertheless required in order to guard fully, explain properly and define efficaciously the very deposit of faith. Truths of this type, therefore, to which dogmatic facts pertain *per se,* inasmuch as the deposit of faith is not able to be preserved and expounded without them, these truths, I say, concern the deposit of faith, not indeed of themselves, but as necessary for guarding that deposit of faith. All Catholic theologians completely agree that the Church, in her authentic proposal and definition of truths of this sort, is infallible, such that to deny this infallibility would be a very grave error. A diversity of opinion turns only on the question of the degree of certitude, i.e., on whether the infallibility in proposing these truths—and therefore in proscribing errors through censures inferior to the note of heresy—should be considered a dogma of faith, so that to deny this infallibility to the Church would be heretical, or whether it is a truth not revealed in itself but one deduced from revealed dogma and as such is only theologically certain.

Now, since what must be said about the infallibility of
the Pope in defining truths is completely the same as what
must be said about the infallibility of the Church defining,
there arises the same question about the extension of pontifical infallibility to those truths not revealed in themselves but
which pertain to the guarding of the deposit of the faith. The
question, I say, arises as to whether papal infallibility in defining these truths is not only theologically certain but is a
dogma of the faith, exactly the same question as has arisen
about the infallibility of the Church. Now, since it has
seemed to members of the Deputation, by unanimous agreement, that this question should not be defined, at least not
now, but should be left in the state in which it presently is, it
necessarily follows, according to the opinion of the same
Deputation, that the decree of faith about the infallibility of
the Roman Pontiff should be seen in such a way that there is
defined, as far as the object of infallibility in definitions of the
Roman Pontiff is concerned, that there must be believed
exactly the same thing as is believed in respect to the object
of infallibility in definitions of the Church. Thus, the present
definition about the object of infallibility contains two parts
which are intimately connected. The first part enunciates the
object of infallibility only generically, namely that it is doctrine of faith and morals. The second part of the definition
distinctly sets forth this object of infallibility, not indeed by
individual considerations, but by circumscribing and determining it by comparing it with the infallibility of the Church
in defining, so that the very same thing must be confessed
about the object of infallibility when the Pope is defining as
must be confessed about the object of infallibility when the
Church is defining. These two parts always have to be taken [1227]
together if the true meaning of our definition is to be
grasped. Therefore not only must it be said that the Pope is
infallible in matters of faith and morals, when he defines doctrines about faith and morals, but that this infallibility is that
infallibility which the Church enjoys. Therefore, someone
who would simply assert that the Roman Pontiff is infallible

when he defines something about faith or morals has by no means comprehended the meaning of our definition. Nor is the meaning of our formula comprehended by someone who simply asserts that the Roman Pontiff is infallible when he defines something which simply must be held by the Church. The two things must always be joined so that the meaning of our formula be correct and true. Moreover, this formula seems most suitable to express both things: "The Roman Pontiff, when he defines a doctrine of faith and morals to be held by the universal Church, enjoys that infallibility with which the divine Redeemer wished His Church to be endowed in defining doctrine of faith or morals."

Therefore, in this entire definition, the following three things are contained: 1) The Roman Pontiff, through the divine assistance promised to him, is infallible, when, by his supreme authority, he defines a doctrine which must be held by the Universal Church, or, as very many theologians say, when he definitively and conclusively proposes his judgment; 2) the object of these infallible definitions is doctrine about faith or morals; 3) in respect to the object of infallibility, generically proposed in this way, the infallibility of the Pope is neither more nor less extensive than is the infallibility of the Church in her definitions of doctrine of faith and morals. Therefore just as everyone admits that to deny the infallibility of the Church in defining dogmas of faith is heretical, so the force of this decree of the Vatican Council makes it no less heretical to deny the infallibility of the supreme Pontiff, considered in itself, when he defines dogmas of faith. However, in respect to those things about which it is theologically certain—but not as yet certain *de fide*—that the Church is infallible, these things are also not defined by this decree of the sacred Council as having to be believed *de fide* in respect to papal infallibility. With the theological certitude which is had that these other objects, apart from dogmas of the faith, fall within the extension of the infallibility which the Church enjoys in her definitions, so, with that same theological certi-

tude, must it be held, now and in the future, that the infallibility of definitions issued by the Roman Pontiff extends to
these same objects.

In point four, which he further subdivides into three sections, Gasser deals with the intricate subject of the extension of
infallibility, i.e., the object of infallibility. He makes the following clarifications:

1. Infallibility has been promised to the Church in order to
"guard and unfold the integral deposit of the faith."

2. Whatever must be said about the object and extension of
the gift of infallibility in relation to the teaching Church as a
whole must also be said, in the same degree, about the object
and extension of papal infallibility. The definition of papal infallibility is so worded as to make this assertion clear.

3. It must be believed that the Church is infallible in defining matters of faith and morals which are revealed, as these are
found in the fonts of revelation, viz., Scripture and Tradition.

4. There are truths, not of themselves revealed, which are
necessary to "fully guard, properly explain and efficaciously
define" those other truths which are revealed. These truths, i.e.,
those not revealed as such but necessary for the defense, explanation and unfolding of the deposit of faith, belong to the sciences
of philosophy, history, the empirical sciences, etc. The theologians generally break these truths down into various categories,
one of which is mentioned by Gasser, viz., *dogmatic facts*. The
usual example of a "dogmatic fact" would be the Church's
ability to determine whether the ideas presented in such and
such a book are, in their true sense as understood in context, in
harmony with or contrary to the deposit of Faith. This kind of a
decision is involved, for example, when the Church condemns a
book. Revelation does not tell us anything about the *Augustinus*
of Cornelius Jansens. Thus, when the Church determines that
there are errors in it against Faith, she is involved in the determination of a dogmatic fact. It should be noted that sometimes the
term "dogmatic fact" is used in a wider sense, such that it would
include the canonization of individual men and women as saints,
the determination of the ecumenicity of a particular council, etc.,
(which truths would be called by others "hagiographical facts"
and "historical facts," etc.). Gasser may be using this wider sense
here. Cf. below, p. 87, note.

5. The Church is infallible in her proposal of such truths as these, for, without the ability to define such truths, it would ultimately be impossible to guard, unfold and define the revealed truths themselves. On the Church's ability to define such truths infallibly, says Gasser, all theologians agree. It would be a very grave error to deny this.

6. However, says Gasser, there remains a question. Has God revealed that such truths as these can be infallibly defined so that, as a consequence, we must believe this with divine faith? Or, is our degree of certitude about the Church's ability to propose such truths infallibly a certitude that rests on a necessary theological conclusion (and thus "theologically certain") and not on the word of God revealing? The answer to these questions is disputed. In other words, that such truths can be infallibly defined is certain, but on what does our certitude rest?

7. Since the nature of the certitude is disputed, it is not the intention of the definition of papal infallibility to determine the question. The definition merely says that, if the Church can do it, so can the Pope. If it is a matter of faith that the Church can propose such truths infallibly, then it is a matter of faith that the Pope can propose such truths infallibly. If it is only theologically certain that the Church can propose such truths infallibly, then it is only theologically certain that the Pope can propose such truths infallibly.

As was true with his explanation of the nature of the act of infallibility, Gasser's explanation of the object or extension of infallibility did not please all the bishops, and so he had to return to this point as well in his final relatio on July 16th. His remarks on that occasion follow:

"The third observation concerns the object of infallibility. I have recently spoken about this matter at great length, but, nevertheless—as the exceptions themselves make manifest—very many of the reverend fathers still seem to be uncertain about the meaning of these words [in the definition]. Therefore they have proposed many new formulas about the object of infallibility. Indeed these formulas frequently consist of two propositions, the first of which is often completely indeterminate, so much so that it refers to all pontifical decrees without any distinction. In the second proposition, the first proposition is, in some way, determined and confined. The Deputation *de fide* is not able to approve such a way of enunciating the matter, but rather prefers by far its own formula already approved by the general congregation. The Deputation's formula sets forth everything in one proposition about the object of infallibility in such a way, however, that it is set forth under a twofold notion, i.e., a generic and specific one.

From the generic notion, i.e., when the Roman Pontiff, exercising his office as supreme pastor and teacher, defines a doctrine of faith and morals which must be held by the universal Church, he is infallible—from this general notion we learn that the Roman Pontiff, speaking *ex cathedra* is infallible when he defines something about matters of faith and morals. But, from the immediately adjoined specific notion we learn that, in the extension of this infallibility, in the application of his infallibility to individual decrees of the Roman Pontiff, a distinction must be made. This distinction teaches indeed that some things (as is also true of dogmatic definitions of councils) are certain *de fide,* such that whoever would deny that the Pontiff had been infallible in issuing such a decree, would, by that very fact of denial, be a heretic, no matter whether he denied or affirmed the doctrine so taught. Other decrees of the Roman Pontiff are indeed also certain as far as infallibility is concerned, but this certitude is not the same, just as in other definitions and decrees of councils there is not the same certitude about the infallibility of the council. This last mentioned certitude is only theological certitude in the sense that whoever would deny that the Church or, equally, the Pope would be infallible in issuing such a decree would not as such be openly a heretic, but nevertheless would commit a most grave error and a very grave sin by erring in this way. Therefore, in our formula we enunciate the whole object of infallibility simultaneously under one proposition, but under a twofold generic and specific notion so that from the generic notion there is evident only the general object of infallibility and then, from the specific notion, there appears the certitude of this infallibility, i.e., whether it is of faith or only theologically certain, etc." *(Mansi,* 52, 1316)

What Gasser meant in his earlier response to Bishop Colet's suggested correction #45 can now be more clearly seen. Having rejected the substitution of "principles of morals" for the phrase "matters of faith and morals," Gasser went on to comment: "Furthermore the principles of morals are able to be other merely philosophical principles of natural moral goodness *(naturalis honestatis),* which do not pertain to the deposit of faith in every respect." There can be, he is saying, some principles of natural morality, not revealed as such, which may not be necessary to "fully guard, properly explain and efficaciously define" the deposit of faith. If there are such, they would not fall under the object of infallibility, and therefore the term "principles of faith and morals" is too vague and imprecise a term to use in the definition of papal infallibility.

In a sense, that earlier response turned the tables on Bishop Colet's suggestion, since Colet explicitly said that he was just seconding the suggestion of Bishop Yusto of Burgos. Now the whole point of Yusto's proposal (cf. *Mansi*, 52, 853-860) was to limit the object of papal infallibility to "general principles of morals" *(idem,* 853). Gasser and the Deputation rejected the terminology in which the suggestion was couched as being too broad while, at the same time, defending an extension of infallibility which went far beyond the mere "general principles of morals" which Yusto and Colet desired.

Part of the difficulty in the entire discussion of the extension or object of infallibility was the fact that the infallibility of the Church herself and the extension of her infallibility had not been directly defined. Vatican I intended to do just that, but, in deciding to treat papal infallibility before completing its proposed constitution on the Church, the Council was faced with the problem of having to explain the Pope's infallibility in reference to the Church's infallibility without having first taught on the latter. Now, as a matter of fact, both the first and second draft of the proposed dogmatic constitution on the Church proposed to teach that the Church's infallibility extended not only to matters of faith and morals revealed by God, but to all the truths needed to explain, guard and define the truths which had been revealed (cf. *Mansi*, 53, 313D, and 316, canon 9 and the alternate version of canon 10). When Joseph Kleutgen presented the second draft of that document to the Deputation *de fide,* he said, among other things: "...the Church is infallible not only in those things which are revealed *per se,* but also in those things which, in some way, cohere with what has been revealed. Therefore in the very definition of infallibility we have written: 'those things which must be held and passed on' and not 'which are defined to be held and passed on as of divine faith.'" *(idem,* 326). (It is to be noted that in the definition of papal infallibility the same terminology is used, viz., "when he defines matters of faith and morals which *must be held,*" not *which must be believed.* The reason for the *tenendam* rather than the *credendum* is surely that given by Kleutgen.) As far as the extension of infallibility and the "matters of morals" was concerned, Kleutgen said: "What we have said generally about the doctrine of faith, must be especially considered in the discipline of morals. The condition of human life is so various and multiform that innumerable questions arise about morals for which we find no answer in revelation itself. And, nevertheless, the Church in her judgment has defined many of these questions, affixing to these evil opinions the censures about which we have spoken.... For, if the Church in proscribing opinions is able to err, what follows except that it would be able to happen that all the faithful would be compelled by the Church, under severe edict and the proposed penalty of excommunication, to embrace errors which corrupt faith and morals?" (*Mansi*, 53, 327)

It is to be noted that Vatican Council II completed the unfinished work of Vatican I in respect to the question of the object or extension of infallibility. In its Dogmatic Constitution *Lumen Gentium*, the bishops at Vatican II taught: "Moreover this infallibility, with which the Divine Redeemer wished His Church to be endowed in defining doctrine of faith or morals extends as far as the deposit of divine Revelation, to guard it religiously and faithfully expound it" (#25). And, in the *Declaration Mysterium Ecclesiae* of June, 1973, the Congregation for the Doctrine of the Faith repeated this teaching in the following words: "According to Catholic doctrine, the infallibility of the Church's Magisterium extends not only to the deposit of faith but also to those matters without which that deposit cannot be rightly preserved and expounded" (Trans. Austin Flannery, O.P., *Vatican Council II*, Costello Pub. Co., Northport, N.Y., 1982, vol. II, p. 432).

Vatican II's teaching is, of course, not a solemn definition, and thus the teaching about the extension of the Church's infallibility remains undefined, since Vatican II, by set purpose, did not define doctrine. Nonetheless, it has moved the issue beyond the place where it was at the time Gasser made his commentary on the object of infallibility and made it formal conciliar teaching. And, according to the dogmatic definition of Vatican I, what must be said of the extension of the infallibility of the Church must also be said of the extension of papal infallibility.

Having finished his remarks on the object of infallibility, Gasser has finished his official presentation of the new formula of the definition itself. The new formula was accepted in the subsequent voting (cf. *Mansi*, 53, 1231). He now moves on to deal briefly with the remaining suggested corrections. His text of July 11 continues:

Now, as to what concerns the method for treating this matter in our voting, most eminent and reverend fathers, you can see for yourselves that everything in our formula is so interconnected that those things which are found in the following suggested corrections—touching upon the object of papal infallibility and on the relation which exists between papal infallibility and the infallibility of the Church—are not able to be joined to our formula, nor can anything be separated from our formula. Therefore there remains nothing to do except first submit to a vote of the most reverend fathers this formula of the Deputation. But if this formula is accepted—as, with the help of God, I hope it will be—then no further votes need be sought in respect to the following suggestions, to the extent that they concern the object of papal infallibility and the relation between papal infallibility and the infallibility of the Church. This is so because, as I have just said, the matter found in these suggestions cannot be taken into our formula while saving its meaning, nor is anything able to be omitted from our formula without ruining its tight connections. Therefore a vote will first be sought in respect to our formula, and, in case it is accepted by the [1228] general congregation, another further relatio about those suggestions concerning the object of infallibility and the relation between papal infallibility and the infallibility of the Church will no longer be necessary. Therefore I think I can refrain from any further observations about these suggestions and only say something if a particular thing seems to be worthy of note.

Suggestion #54 is the first about which a vote will not be sought, presuming that our formula is accepted.

Suggestion #55. Likewise, no vote will be sought for this suggestion because the reverend father wants that the Pope be declared infallible not only in defining but even in seeking the truth.

Suggestion #56 will not be voted upon. The same is true for suggestions #57 and #58. But the reason for not seeking a vote in these cases is different. The reverend father agrees with the previous suggestion which wants that "matters of morals" be replaced by "principles of morals." Therefore, since it has already been said that this suggestion could not be accepted and would not be submitted to a vote, so also no vote will be sought in this case.

Suggestion #59 agrees with the former, and therefore no vote will be asked.

Suggestion #60 wants an addition which does not pertain to a dogmatic constitution, i.e., concerning the promulgation of pontifical definitions through the bishops. This does not concern a dogmatic constitution and therefore no vote will be sought.

Suggestion #61 will not require a vote, presuming our formula is approved.

Suggestion #62 deals with offering assent to papal decrees of faith. The Deputation thinks that this suggestion should also not be accepted by the general congregation. For this suggestion belongs to a system different from our own, because this suggestion only finds its place if it is supposed that the assent of the Church, whether antecedent or consequent, is necessary. Since we have already not excluded the cooperation of the Church, we do not exclude the consent of the Church as long as this cooperation and this consent are not set forth as a condition without which the Pontiff is not able to be infallible. As I have said, in our system this suggestion does not find a place and therefore should not be accepted.

Suggestion #63 is also not to be submitted for a vote, presuming the acceptance, etc.

Suggested corrections #56 and #57 are covered by the new formula of the definition. Suggested correction #58 is the suggestion of Bishop Yusto of Burgos, about which enough has been said above when treating of the extension or object of infallibility. Suggested correction #59 is another of Bishop Colet's, seconding the previous one of Bishop Yusto.

Suggestion #64 for like reason will not be submitted to a vote although the proposal is nevertheless satisfied by our new formula, although not in the exact sense of the suggestion.

Suggestion #65 will likewise not be submitted for a vote. The reverend father sets forth many—and certainly not to be spurned—matters of gravity which propose that the Pope is infallible even in those things which he defines and proposes to be rejected with a censure less than heresy. But the observation which I gave in commenting on the definition is valid in respect to these matters.

Suggestion #66. No vote will be sought because the desire of the reverend father is partly satisfied through the inserted paragraph and partly because it contains certain things about the object of papal infallibility which are not in harmony with our formula.

Suggestion #67 will also not be submitted for a vote.

Suggestion #68 is, as far as its substance, the same as that which was newly adopted by the Deputation and which we have in our formula.

[1229]   Suggestion #69 will not be presented for a vote, presuming the acceptance, etc.

Suggestion #70. The reverend father wants certain things to be added at the end of the definition, viz., "The obligation remaining firm by which Catholics, etc." But this definition is not opportune lest we seem to anticipate the

---

Suggested correction #66 was made by Bishop Martin of Paderborn, a member of the Deputation *de fide*. He wanted to omit the parallel drawn between the infallibility of the Church and that of the Pope (cf. *Mansi*, 52, 939-940).

Suggested correction #68 was submitted by Cullen of Dublin and is almost the same as the new formula sponsored by the Deputation.

Suggested correction #70 was another of Yusto of Burgos with the purpose of reminding the faithful that they are obliged to adhere to the papal magisterium even when the Pope has not defined something as of faith *(Mansi*, 52, 1135).

judgment of the sacred Council. Furthermore, in some way it is already provided for in the first dogmatic constitution which treats of the faith.

Suggestion #71 will not be submitted for a vote because it wants to extend our definition even to dogmatic facts, and do that not even in the same sense which I set forth in the commentary on our definition.

Suggestion #72. Likewise no vote will be sought for this suggestion as far as its first part. The same holds true of the second part because it also treats of the object of faith. Indeed the reverend father wants that it be expressly defined that the infallibility of the Roman Pontiff and the Church are the same. In what sense this is said by us has already been explained in the commentary on our formula. Therefore this suggestion will not be put to a vote.

There now follow certain things to be added after the definition and before the canons. As far as all these warnings which have been put forth by very many fathers are concerned, the Deputation *de fide* thinks these warnings have been sufficiently satisfied in the paragraph newly inserted between the first and second paragraphs. Therefore all these suggestions are rejected by the Deputation, without, however, anticipating the judgment of the general congregation at least as far as some of these suggestions go.

Therefore, suggestion #73 is indeed not recommended by the Deputation *de fide,* but there will be a vote on it nevertheless. The reverend father wants that it be said that in the future, councils will not become useless, etc.

The same is true of suggestion #74. For this one no vote will be asked because it does not contain a properly worded suggestion.

Suggested correction #71 was made by Bishop Peter Maupas from Dalmatia who wanted the definition to speak of *facta historica* (cf. *Mansi,* 52, 839). Since Gasser speaks of *facta dogmatica* in his response, we can assume that here and above, when speaking of the extension of infallibility, Gasser uses *facta dogmatica* in its loose or wide sense.

Suggestion #75. According to the mind of the Deputation this suggestion is already provided for in the inserted paragraph and thus it can be voted on but the Deputation *de fide* does not recommend it.

The same holds true for suggestion #76 which asks that it be expressly stated that the impeccability of the Pope is not included in the definition on infallibility.

As far as suggestions #77 and 78 are concerned. These suggestions or rather these warnings will not be put to a vote because the reverend authors who are members of the Deputation *de fide* agree that their proposals are abundantly provided for in the inserted paragraph. Therefore there will be no vote on #77 and 78.

Now we come to #79 or to the canons. As far as this last part is concerned, I will deal with it briefly if the reverend fathers permit me. Much has been disputed and discussed about this matter in the Deputation *de fide*, but all are in agreement that no canon found in the following suggestions can be accepted. And the reason for this, as I will explain briefly, is the following: In a canon the following things are required: 1) that the doctrine of the chapter be repeated in the canon as far as its substance and substantial points; 2) that a canon be directly opposed to errors raging against this doctrine. Therefore a canon which should be approved, in order that it may be proposed to the general congregation for approval, should contain those things which I have just indicated.

[1230] In reality no [suggested] canon contains all these requirements, but rather lacks one or the other. Even in those which are certainly very good—and especially in two suggestions which much occupied the minds of the Deputation— even there the doctrine is not repeated as far as its full substance, but is, if I may speak thus, essentially changed. For the doctrine as it was found in the old proposed chapter which was discussed in the general congregations, consisted of two parts. The first part said that, when the Pope defined a matter of faith, it had to be held that then the Pope was infallible; the second part said that the infallibility of the

Pope and Church is the same and that, therefore, the infallibility of the Pope extended to the same object as did the infallibility of the Church. But no canon integrally refers to this whole doctrine in each of its parts and therefore in its substantial elements.

As far as the opposed errors are concerned: indeed there would be some canons which would proscribe the error which says that papal decrees are reformable. But this matter has already been treated in our formula and, once the definition is issued as it is set forth in our new proposed chapter or in our new formula, there can be no room for this error. But indeed another error should be proscribed, namely one that would say that the decrees of the Roman Pontiff are not irreformable and are not to be held if the assent of the Church has not accrued to them or if it is not clear that such assent has accrued. Therefore, since no canon corresponds to the things which are required if we come down to the singular and special, the Deputation, after long discussion, thought it wise to propose to the general congregation a general canon, that is, the last words of our former proposed chapter now immediately joined in the form of a canon to the doctrine of the newly proposed chapter. This canon, therefore, reads as follows: "If anyone should presume to contradict this definition of ours—may God prevent such—let such a one be anathema."

As has been said, the recommendations of the Deputation, as set forth by Gasser, were followed by the bishops in the voting. Significant questioning was raised in respect to only a few items. They were: 1) the meaning of the word "define" and 2) the matter of the object or extension of infallibility. With these we have dealt above. The third major question concerned the words "...nor were they ignorant of the fact that it is necessary that every church...and Roman Church perseveringly holds, together with the other churches" which were found in the Corrections proposed by the Deputation on July 9 (cf. above, p. 11) and were a kind of combined citation of St. Irenaeus and St. Augustine. There was much feeling that they were taken out of

Most eminent and reverend fathers, I have had these things to set before you. As far as the manner of treating them goes, the vote will first be asked about that canon just proposed and which was not printed but which you now have before your eyes. As far as the other proposed canons go, they will be presented for a vote lest the liberty of the council seem to be prejudiced. Nevertheless the Deputation *de fide* cannot make any of these proposed canons its own.

Having said this, most eminent and reverend fathers, I beg your pardon if I have said anything which is unfavorable or if, by chance, charity has been wounded. Certainly such was not my intention. There remains only one thing and I ask it, viz., that finally an end be put to that sad period which began with the great schism of the Western Church in the 16th century and which extends to our own times. Indeed this period began (all know the causes of this event) with the

---

their original context and should be withdrawn from the proposed insertion. In his final relatio on July 16, Gasser vigorously defended the appropriateness of the citations, but announced that the Deputation would withdraw them *(Mansi, 52, 1314-1315)*. The fourth and last question concerned a desire by some of the bishops that the definition explicitly state that the Pope's infallible decisions did not depend on the consent of the Church. Gasser replied on July 16 that such an insertion would be redundant since the phrase "irreformable of themselves" meant just that. However, he also announced that the Deputation acceded to the request and would add the words "and not from the consent of the Church" after "irreformable of themselves." Thus was the work on Chapter IV of the Dogmatic Constitution *Pastor Aeternus* completed. The entire constitution was formally voted upon in public session on July 18, 1870, 533 in favor, 2 against. Some eighty-eight bishops had voted against the constitution in the private vote held on July 13. Most of these left Rome for their home dioceses before the final public voting. All afterwards assented to the constitution and promulgated it in their dioceses, Bishop Hefele of Rottenburg being among the last to do so. Gasser's expressed fears had not been realized: a very great cause had not been ruined by its advocate. Quite the contrary.

putting down of the authority of the Roman Pontiff and has arrived at the point that all authority, both sacred and secular, inasmuch as it descends from a divine origin and from the grace of God, is now spurned by many and completely left out of consideration by many more.... Let us therefore put an end to this epoch, lifting up once again the authority of the Roman Pontiff to that eminence it had in this regard before it was so greatly disputed.

Footnotes

1. *Defens. declarat. cleri Gallicani* (lib. X), cap. VI.
2. *De auctorit. papae et concilii* cap. IX et XI.
3. *Lib. VI,* cap. VII.
4. *Epist. 53* alias 165, #2 (Migne, P.L. XXXIII, 196).
5. *Epist. ad Damasum papam* (Migne, P.L. XXII, 356).
6. *Enarr. in ps. XL, n. 30* (Migne, P.L. XIV, 1082).
7. *Lib. III, adv. Rufinum* cap. XV (Migne, P.L. XXIII, 468).
8. *Cozza hist. polem de Graecor. schismate* tom. II, part. IV, cap. XXVIII, n. 1218.
9. Labbe, *Collect. concil.,* tom XVIII, col. 1154 et seqq., edit. venet. Coleti.
10. *Contr. Iulian.,* lib. II, n. CIII (Migne, P.L. XLV, 1183).
11. Labbe, *Collect. concil.,* tom. VII, col. 758, edit. venet. Coleti.
12. Inter opp. s. Leonis, tom. I, epist. CXX ad Theodoret. episc. Cyri, pag. 1219, edit. Baller.

The Infallibility of
The Churdh's Magisterium

John Henry Newman, a contemporary of Bishop Gasser and one who did not think it "opportune" to define the infallibility of the Pope, wrote the following oft-quoted words on infallibility in his famous *An Essay on the Development of Christian Doctrine* in its 1878 edition:

> "The common sense of mankind does but support a conclusion forced upon us by analogical considerations. It feels that the very idea of revelation implies a present informant and guide, and that an infallible one....
>
> "Surely, either an objective revelation has not been given, or it has been provided with means for impressing its objectiveness on the world. If Christianity be a social religion, as it certainly is, and if it be based on certain ideas acknowledged as divine, or a creed...and if these ideas have various aspects and make distinct impressions on different minds..., what power will suffice to meet and to do justice to these conflicting conditions but a supreme authority ruling and reconciling individual judgments by a divine right and a recognized wisdom? ...Philosophy, taste, prejudice, passion, party, caprice will find no common measure, unless there be some supreme power to control the mind and to compel agreement. There can be no combination on the basis of truth without an organ of truth."[1]

Newman's argument has lost none of its cogency. Indeed, in face of a contemporary challenge to the Church's prerogatives in proclaiming the truth, Pope John Paul II has restated Newman's thought in an interesting series of rhetorical phrases:

> Since Christ bestowed on the Church everything indispensable for carrying out the mission entrusted to her, could He hold back from her the gift of certainty about the truths she knows and proclaims?
>
> Above all, could He withhold this gift from those who, succeeding Peter and the apostles as shepherds and teachers, inherited therewith a special responsibility for the community of the faithful?
>
> Precisely because human beings are fallible, would it be possible for Christ, while desiring to preserve the Church in truth, to leave her shepherds and bishops, and especially Peter and his successors, without the gift by means of which He would assure the infallible teaching of the truths of faith and the true principles of morality?[2]

Either God has revealed Himself to us, giving us a lasting message of truth, and provided that this truth be preserved secure and certain through an office capable of teaching the truth without error, or He has not revealed Himself at all, at least not definitively and once and for all in Christ. "There can be no combination on the basis of truth without an organ of truth." This organ of truth the Catholic Church claims as existing in the teaching function of the bishops united with the successor of Peter, a teaching office or organ of truth called in recent centuries "the *Magisterium*." Newman's words concerning its function strike our ears harshly. He asserts that its role is to "control the mind and to compel agreement." By this, of course, he does not mean the type of "mind control" with which, especially since his time, we have become so familiar and rightly reject: psychological manipulation often aided by physical torture and/or drugs. He was thinking of an office which would speak with an authority claiming to be supported by God's own, an office guaranteed as free from error in all its definitive utterances. It would be, therefore, an office which would "control and compel" by the very power of manifest truth—even when it cannot, as in the case of revealed supernatural truth, be fully comprehended—to attract, order and give peace to the human mind which is constantly plagued by the insecurity caused by conflicting claims, a near infinite variety of opinions and its own intellectual and psychological weakness.

The citations from Newman and Pope John Paul II remind us of a truth frequently mentioned by Gasser in his *relatio* to the bishops at Vatican Council, viz., that infallibility is a *gift* bestowed by God on His Church. It functions, therefore, in the order of grace, of charism, and, in particular, of a grace given to some for the sake of others (*gratia gratis data* as the theologians call such manifestations of God's favor). It is, for the Catholic who has the Spirit-given ability to recognize this gift of infallibility in the Church, a motive of appreciation and love for the Church and for the Church's Lord. It is the gift of infallibility which brings the words of Christ to us pure and unadulterated, which preserves His truth and sews it unmixed in the world, gives us certitude and thus nourishes our hope.

> It is hard to imagine where the Gospel would have got to or in what state it would have reached us if, *per impossible,* it had not been composed, preserved and commented on within the great Catholic community— hard to picture the deformation and mutilation it would have suffered both as to text and as to interpretation...history speaks forcefully enough. There is no counting the number of aberrations which have been based upon an appeal to the Gospel, or the number of those who have, in consequence of them, toppled over into "atheistic and impious doctrines, or stupid and ridiculous beliefs."
>
> We owe our praise, therefore, to this great Mother of ours for the divine mystery which she communicates to us.... This chaste Mother pours into us and sustains a faith which is always whole and which neither human decadence nor spiritual lassitude can touch, however deep they may go.... This wise Mother steers us clear of sectarian excesses and the deceptive enthusiasm which

is always followed by revulsion; she teaches us to love all that is good, all that is true, all that is just, and to reject nothing that has not been tested.... She scatters the darkness in which men either slumber or despair or—pitifully—"shape as they please their fantasies of the infinite." Without discouraging us from any task she protects us from the deceptive myths of the Churches made by the hand of man...she is initiated into His secrets and teaches us whatever pleases Him.[3]

Newman, because of the times in which he lived, emphasized, like Gasser and Vatican Council I, only one aspect of the gift of infallibility, viz., the infallible prerogative of one part of the Church's teaching office or Magisterium. Like Gasser, of course, Newman—and all other Catholic theologians—realized that papal infallibility was only a facet of the total gift of infallibility with which Christ had endowed His Church. It is only in our own day, however, thanks to the work of the Second Council of the Vatican, that the Church in her teaching has given us a more comprehensive picture of infallibility than that provided by Vatican I. In that wider picture, Gasser's *relatio* and Vatican I's definition of papal infallibility lose none of their significance. Indeed, there is much in Gasser's *relatio* which can contribute to an adequate understanding of Vatican II's teaching on the Church's gift of infallibility. Just as Vatican II puts papal infallibility and Gasser's *relatio* in a wider perspective, so papal infallibility and the *relatio* of Gasser which explains what the bishops at Vatican I intended by their definition, help make concrete and delineate the teachings of Vatican II. In order for the relationship of the two councils to be better seen, we must look briefly at the whole area of ecclesial infallibility as presented by Vatican II.

Before beginning, however, a definition of terms might be helpful. Thus, following Gasser and Vatican I, we define infallibility as that special gift of God which enables the Catholic Church to hold and propose without error those truths which God intends to be known and held for the sake of our salvation. Furthermore, any discussion of infallibility can be conveniently broken down into two headings: the subject of infallibility and the object of infallibility. By *subject of infallibility* theology proposes to answer the question, "Who is infallible?" By *object of infallibility* theology proposes—as already seen in the commentary of Gasser's *relatio* (cf. pp. 75ff. above)—to answer the question, "What aspects of the truth are covered by the gift of infallibility—everything or only what God has directly revealed?" We shall now consider these questions in turn.

I. The subject of infallibility

As Bishop Gasser noted in his *relatio* to the bishops at Vatican I, only God is absolutely infallible (cf. p. 45 above). He alone is totally incapable of error of any kind. Thus, when one asks the question, "Who is infallible?" one is not expecting the only obvious and completely correct answer. In fact, the question is asked within a context which means, "Understanding that God has endowed the Church with a charism of freedom from error, who in the Church may be said to exercise this charism?" Or, another and not exactly identical way of putting the question: where can infallibility be said to reside?

1. All infallibility is rooted in the gift which God gives to His Church as a whole. Thus, we speak of the *infallibility of the whole People of God*. The Second Vatican Council proposes this doctrine in the following words of *Lumen Gentium* (the *Dogmatic Constitution on the Church*): "The holy People of God also participates in the prophetic office of Christ, especially by diffusing a living testimony to Him through a life of faith and love, by offering Him the sacrifice of praise, the fruit of lips confessing His Name (cf. Heb. 13:15). The universal body of the faithful *(universitas fidelium)* who have an anointing from the Spirit (cf. 1 Jn. 2:20, 27), cannot err in believing, and the universal body of the faithful manifests this particular property it possesses when, 'from the bishops to the last members of the laity' it exhibits

its universal consent about matters of faith and morals by means of a supernatural sense of the faith which belongs to the whole people. Indeed, by this sense of the faith which is stirred up and sustained by the Spirit of truth, the People of God, under the leadership of the sacred Magisterium to which it faithfully submits, truly receives not the word of men but rather the word of God (cf. 1 Th. 2:13), clings without error to the faith once handed on to the saints (cf. Jude 3), penetrates it more profoundly by correct judgments and applies it more fully to life" *(Lumen Gentium,* 12).

The first and fundamental *subject* of infallibility is, therefore, the entire People of God, the Church. And, in a real sense it is this understanding of infallibility which is the most important. With this aspect of the gift of infallibility there is connected the frequently abused notion of the *sensus fidelium,* the "sense of the faithful," or that which the Council in the paragraph quoted above refers to with the words "supernatural sense of the faith." It is clear from the teaching of Vatican II that the gift of infallibility resides in the *sensus fidelium.* The body of the faithful cannot err in matters of faith and morals. It must be noted, however, that this infallibility of the People of God is given to the entire body of the faithful, that is to the Pope and bishops as well as to the general faithful. It is not given to the faithful in contradistinction to the infallible charism given to the Magisterium of Pope and bishops. Indeed, the proper exercise of the infallibility of the entire People of God necessitates a "faithful submission to the sacred Magisterium," if that people is to believe, penetrate more deeply and apply more thoroughly the faith entrusted to the saints. If the teaching of the Pope and bishops is not included in the "universal consent about matters of faith and morals," then one does not truly have a *sensus fidelium,* a consensus among all the faithful. Once that is clear, it should be obvious that determining the *sensus fidelium* is not a matter of poll-taking or of sociological reports. In this regard we may cite again Cardinal Newman, that great exponent of the *consensus fidelium* from his work *On Consulting the Faithful in Matters of Doctrine:*

> I think I am right in saying that the tradition of the Apostles, committed to the whole Church in its various constituents and functions *per modum unius,* manifests itself variously at various times: sometimes by the mouth of the episcopacy, sometimes by the doctors, sometimes by the people, sometimes by liturgies, rites, ceremonies, and customs, by events, disputes, movements, and all those other phenomena which are comprised under the name of history. It follows that none of these channels of tradition may be treated with disrespect; granting at the same time fully, that the gift of discerning, discriminating, defining, promulgating, and enforcing any portion of that tradition resides in the *Ecclesia docens.*[4]

Certainly the *episcopal college* (i.e., the *moral* majority of the bishops united with the head of the college, the Bishop of Rome) has never fallen away from the faith or taught error. Nevertheless, there have been times in history when great numbers of bishops have fallen away from the true faith and even taught error. One need only think of the period between the Council of Nicea (325) and Constantinople I (381) when, for various motives, many bishops taught or tolerated Arian or semi-Arian doctrine. Or of the bishops of England during the reigns of Henry VIII and his son Edward.

There have been times in the history of the Church when her great theologians and doctors have erred in matters of faith. One need only consider the views of St. Bernard, St. Albert the Great, St. Thomas Aquinas and others concerning the Immaculate Conception of Our Lady. To exculpate them, one may say in truth that the Church had not yet formally taught this truth. However, what is at question is not formal orthodoxy. They certainly all willed fidelity to the truth. What is involved is the question of their mistake in a matter of truth, for the Immaculate Conception of Mary was as true in the 12th and 13th century as it was in the 19th and 20th. Furthermore, it was a truth already perceived by the piety of many of the *ordinary* lay Catholics of those ages.

There have been times, too, when vast numbers of the lay members of the Church have erred in faith (admittedly, often led into such error by members of the hierarchy). One need only think of the Albigensian heresy of the 13th century, or of the large numbers of Catholics who abandoned the teaching of the Catholic Church during the major periods of schism and heresy.

Indeed, when one looks carefully at the history of the Catholic Church, there can be discerned periods when various elements of the Catholic Body have *combined* to hold erroneous views. At times, bishops and laity; at other times, theologians and laity; yet again, bishops and theologians. Never, however, has the body of the faithful as a whole, the *universitas fidelium* spoken of by Vatican Council II, combined to reject what it formerly knew to be true or to agree upon a novelty which was in fact erroneous.

This gift of infallibility as given to the entire Body of the Faithful is sometimes compared with the mark of *indefectibility* by which the Church, as a whole, is rendered immune from the danger of falling away from the Faith. As explained by some theologians, the mark of *indefectability* would be consistent with temporary lapses of the entire body of the Church from true faith. Such an understanding of *indefectability* would, of course, differentiate it essentially from the gift of infallibility. In fact, however, as understood in the Catholic Church, indefectability would exclude a falling away of the whole body of the faithful in general and such an understanding makes the notion practically identical with that gift of infallibility possessed by the entire Church as that gift is propounded by Vatican Council II.

2. Commenting on the remarkable unity shown by the various parts of the entire People of God in adhering to and understanding the Faith, Vatican Council II's Dogmatic Constitution on Divine Revelation *(Dei Verbum)* said:

> Sacred Tradition and Sacred Scripture constitute the one sacred deposit of the word of God entrusted to the Church. Adhering to this deposit the entire holy people, united with its pastors perseveres unceasingly

in the doctrine of the Apostles and in fellowship, in the breaking of the bread and in prayers (cf. Acts 2:42), so that, in holding on to the Faith which has been handed down, and in living it and professing it, there may be a singular meeting of the minds *(singularis conspiratio)* of the bishops and the faithful (# 10).

The same document notes immediately, however, that the duty of authentically or authoritatively teaching that same Faith belongs not to all the People of God in general but to the Magisterium of the Pope and bishops.

The duty, however, of authentically interpreting the word of God, whether written or handed down, has been given only to the living Magisterium of the Church whose authority is exercised in the name of Jesus Christ.[5]

This special duty of teaching authentically in the name of Christ has manifested itself in the life of the Church from the earliest days and becomes especially evident in the work of the bishops in the great ecumenical councils from Nicea (325 A.D.) to Vatican II. Pope Pius XII briefly summarized the whole of Catholic Tradition on this special role of the Pope and bishops when he said, "Besides the lawful successors of the Apostles, namely the Roman Pontiff for the Universal Church and bishops for the faithful entrusted to their care, there are no other teachers divinely constituted in the Church of Christ."[6] Vatican Council II would put the magisterium of the bishops in a wider context by noting that, although having no jurisdictional duty in respect to the entire Church, all the bishops, together with the Roman Pontiff, have a certain responsibility for the entire Church.

Individual bishops, who are in charge of particular churches, exercise their pastoral rule over the portion of the People of God committed to them and not over the other churches nor over the entire Church. But, as members of the episcopal college and legitimate successors of the Apostles, the individual bishop, by the institution and command of Christ, is held to exercise that solicitude for the universal Church, which, although not by an act of jurisdiction, contributes so greatly to the welfare of the Church universal *(Lumen Gentium,* #23).

Very high among the tasks involved in the general solicitude for the Church universal which is incumbent on all the bishops as members of the episcopal college is the task of teaching the Gospel. Citing the Council of Trent, Vatican II teaches:

> The preaching of the Gospel holds an eminent place among the special duties of bishops. For the bishops are the heralds of the Faith who lead new disciples to Christ; they are authentic doctors or ones enriched by the authority of Christ who preach to the people entrusted to them the Faith to be believed and the morals to be lived *(Lumen Gentium,* no. 25). As successors of the Apostles, the bishops receive from the Lord, to whom all power in heaven and earth has been given, the mission of teaching all nations and of preaching the Gospel to every creature so that all mankind may attain salvation through faith, baptism and the fulfilling of the commandments *(Idem,* no. 24).

The Pope, as Bishop of Rome and head of the College of Bishops, and the bishops fulfill their duty to evangelize in various ways. This teaching role is generally exercised on a day to day basis in the individual dioceses throughout the world, whereby the bishops—including the Bishop of Rome —by their sermons, homilies, pastoral letters, press conferences and the like do their best to spread the message of Christ. This day to day carrying out of the bishops' magisterial office is called the *Ordinary Magisterium* of the Church. Along with all the various groupings which share in the prophetic role of Christ to spread the truth—the example and training given by parents to children, the preaching of priests and deacons, the teaching of religious educators at the various educational levels, the work of theologians, etc.—and which operate under and in harmony with the bishops, the Ordinary Magisterium is the fundamental instrument for preserving, defending and spreading the Faith.

The Ordinary Magisterium of the Pope and bishops together shares in the gift of infallibility given by Christ to the entire People of God. Moreover, the Ordinary Magisterium can express the unerring faith of the entire People of God by an *infallible exercise* of its teaching office. Vatican Council II teaches this explicitly when it says:

> Although the individual bishops do not enjoy the prerogative of infallibility, they do, nevertheless, enunciate the doctrine of Christ infallibly when, even dispersed around the world but preserving the bond of communion between themselves and with the Successor of Peter, they concur on one judgment as having to be held definitively, while authentically teaching on matters of faith and morals *(Lumen Gentium,* no. 25).

Although—as we have seen above when commenting on Bishop Gasser's *relatio*—the First Vatican Council never *directly* defined the infallibility of the Ordinary Magisterium, it had intended to do so in its proposed constitution *On the Church* and actually did so—at least implicitly—in part of its dogmatic constitution *Dei Filius.* In that document the Pope and bishops at Vatican I defined:

> Indeed all those things must be believed by divine and Catholic Faith which are contained in the word of God, written or handed down, and which are proposed by the Church—either by solemn judgment or by the ordinary and universal magisterium—to be believed as being divinely revealed *(Dei Filius,* cap. 3; DS 3011).

Several things are to be noted about the infallible exercise of the Ordinary Magisterium of the Church.

1. It is an expression of the gift of infallibility given to the entire Church, but is *exercised* only by the bishops in union with the Pope and not by the entire People of God. While the "universitas fidelium" enjoys the gift of infallibility, only the Magisterium of Pope and bishops speaks or teaches definitively for the entire Church.

2. The Ordinary Magisterium is only being exercised infallibly when the Pope and bishops, in communion with

one another, express a common judgment on matters of faith and morals as a judgment which *must be held definitively (sententiam tanquam definitive tenendam)*.

3. This infallibility of the Ordinary Magisterium is limited to "matters of faith and morals." What this means specifically we shall see below when considering the question about the object of infallibility.

By the nature of the case it will often be difficult to determine what in fact is being taught infallibly by the Ordinary Magisterium of the Church. This is so because it must be determined that the bishops of the world, in union with the Bishop of Rome, are teaching a matter of faith or morals *which must be held definitively*. It is not, therefore, sufficient to establish that such and such a matter is being taught by the bishops and the Pope. It must be clear that they are teaching it *definitively* as something which *must* be held. Therefore, one must ascertain 1) what exactly is being taught; 2) whether the Pope and bishops are all (i.e., by a *moral* unanimity) teaching it; and 3) what degree of certitude they are attaching to their teaching. All of this entails a somewhat exhaustive study and one in which it can be expected that the experts (i.e., the theologians) will not always come to a meeting of minds. It is such inherent difficulty which leads many to undervalue the Ordinary Magisterium as a source in ascertaining the infallible nature of a dogmatic truth. This is unfortunate for several reasons:

a) It undermines what is truly the *ordinary* manner in which the Faith is preached and passed down in the Tradition of the Church.

b) It has given the impression that the faithful *must* believe or hold only what has been expressly *defined* by the Pope or by an ecumenical Council of the Church, forgetting that, by definition, these are *extraordinary* manifestations of the Magisterium.

c) It is capable of leaving the impression that, when a Pope or Council *defines* a doctrine, they have given to the doctrine a degree of certitude it previously lacked. In reality this is not normally the case. Most doctrines defined by a

Pope, or Pope and council, have previously been part of the infallible teaching of the Ordinary Magisterium. Indeed, part of the purpose of the consultations carried out by Pius IX and Pius XII previous to the definitions of the dogmas of the Immaculate Conception and bodily Assumption of Our Lady was to determine what was already being definitively taught by the Ordinary Magisterium as well as what was believed by the "universitas fidelium" in its own infallible instinct for the truth. While it is clear from the teachings of Vatican Council I and Vatican II that no juridical obligations entailing previous consultation or subsequent approbation can be placed on the Pope or a council in respect to defining infallibly a matter of faith or morals (cf. pp. 42ff. above), it can be said with certitude that such actions of the *extraordinary* Magisterium would be lacking their proper foundation were they not seen in the context of the gift of infallibility given to the entire People of God and to the Ordinary Magisterium when it meets the above-mentioned conditions for an infallible proclamation of the Faith.

3. We next come to the infallible teaching of truth by the *Extraordinary Magisterium* of the Church. This extraordinary Magisterium is exercised in two ways: by the bishops of the world gathered in general or ecumenical Council and/or by the Pope, as Supreme Teacher of the Church and Head of the College of Bishops, defining a doctrine by virtue of the prerogative given to him as Successor of St. Peter.

a) The authority of the College of Bishops gathered in Council to teach infallibly, while never explicitly defined by the Church, is implicitly defined by Vatican Council I in the excerpt from its Constitution *Dei Filius* quoted above; is taught by Vatican Council II in #25 of *Lumen Gentium;* is consonant with the faith and obedience given to the dogmatic definitions of general councils by the Catholic world since the Council of Nicea in 325; and is summarized this way by the new Code of Canon Law:

> The College of Bishops also enjoys infallibility in its teaching when the bishops exercise their magisterium

having come together in an Ecumenical Council and when, as teachers and judges of faith and morals, they definitively declare for the universal Church a doctrine which must be held concerning faith and morals (Canon 749, 2).

As is clear from the nature of the College of Bishops and from the history of the Church, such extraordinary exercises of episcopal infallibility must be carried out in union with the Pope as head of the College or at least have his subsequent approval. Vatican II puts it this way:

> The infallibility promised to the Church is also present in the body of bishops when it exercises its supreme magisterium together with the Successor of Peter. Moreover, to such definitions the assent of the Church is never able to be lacking because of the action of the same Holy Spirit by which the whole flock of Christ is preserved and advances in unity of faith (*Lumen Gentium,* no. 25). (The official footnote here refers to column 1214 of Gasser's *relatio.)*

b) The authority of the Pope to teach infallibly, already defined as a doctrine of the faith by Vatican I, was reaffirmed by the Second Vatican Council in the following words.

> Moreover this infallibility with which the Divine Redeemer wished His Church to be endowed in defining doctrine of faith or morals...is that infallibility which the Roman Pontiff, Head of the College of bishops, enjoys by virtue of his office, when, as supreme pastor and teacher of all of Christ's faithful and the one who confirms his brothers in the faith (cf. Lk. 22:32), he proclaims by a definitive act doctrine concerning faith or morals. Therefore his definitions are rightly called irreformable of themselves and not from the consent of the Church because they are pronounced under the assistance of the Holy Spirit, promised to him in Blessed Peter, and therefore need no approval of others nor do they admit of appeal to any other judgment. For then the Roman Pontiff is pronouncing judgment not as a private person but, as supreme teacher of the universal Church in whom the charism of infallibility belonging to the whole Church

is individually present, he is setting forth or defending a doctrine of Catholic faith *(Lumen Gentium,* no. 25). [The official footnote here refers to column 1213 of Gasser's commentary.]

It is clear that the teaching of Vatican II on papal infallibility is practically a verbatim résumé of the definition of the First Vatican Council (cf. pp. 13-15 and 65ff. above). The infallibility promised by Christ to the entire Church is individually present in the Successor of Peter who acts not as a private person but as supreme teacher of the entire Church. Vatican II inserts into its teaching at this point a reference to the Pope as "Head of the College of Bishops," something not specifically mentioned in Vatican I. It may be inferred from this that a papal definition of faith is, in some way, a collegial act, i.e., an act of the College of Bishops, by way of what we could call an "executive decision." The Pope individually is able to act for the entire college of bishops in such an act and do so without previous consultation or subsequent approbation. This infallibility is exercised when the Pope "proclaims by a definitive act doctrine concerning faith and morals." Vatican II's use of the word "proclaims" *(proclamat)* is significant here. It does not use the word "define." At Vatican I, some of the bishops objected to the use of the word "define" claiming that it was too restrictive and too juridical, implying the use of a specific formula or limiting the Pope to putting an end to a controversy which had arisen about something which was already a matter of faith. The word was accepted only after Bishop Gasser had assured the bishops that the word "define" was not to be understood in a juridical sense but rather "signifies that the Pope directly and conclusively pronounces his sentence about a doctrine which concerns matters of faith or morals and does so in such a way that each one of the faithful can be certain of the mind of the Apostolic See, of the mind of the Roman Pontiff; in such a way, indeed, that he or she knows for certain that such and such a doctrine is held to be heretical, proximate to heresy, certain or erroneous, etc., by the Roman Pontiff" (cf. above, pp. 73-75). By substituting the word "proclaims" for "defines" Vatican II has, in effect, answered the objections of those bishops at Vatican I who wanted some other word substituted for "defines." Closely following Gasser's explanation, however, Vatican II immediately shows that it considers the words "define" and "proclaim" equivalent by using the word "definition" when it states: "Therefore his definitions are rightly called irreformable, etc." In this way, Vatican II also repeats the teaching of Vatican I which asserted that a papal definition of faith is entirely free, an act not limited by antecedent or consequent juridical norms. Although the Pope is *morally* bound to do everything prudently necessary to prepare for a definition of faith, there is no juridical necessity for him to prepare the definition in any specific way, nor is his definition once proclaimed subject to review or approval by the other bishops or the faithful (cf. pages 40-53 and 66ff. above). His judgment will be guaranteed infallible by the action of the Holy Spirit, and that same Spirit will bring it about that the faithful will assent to the papal definition of what must be held as a matter of faith or morals. It may be significant to note that neither Vatican I nor Vatican II says anything about how soon after the papal definition the assent of the whole Church will be evident. History reveals that definitions of faith or morals made either by a Council or by the Pope are often not met with an assent on the part of all, nor with an assent which is immediately manifest. Lack of communications, a failure to preach the definition properly, particular historical circumstances, as well as ignorance and bad will, are all factors which can impede the *manifestation* of the work of the Holy Spirit in assuring assent to an infallible doctrine. Among those who are faithful, however, the assent is present from the beginning, will gradually convince those weaker in faith, and finally visibly manifest itself. Thus, although not specifically mentioned, the passage of time is often a factor when one is searching for signs of the general acceptance of a doctrine.

Before concluding this section on the "subject of infallibility," i.e., on who possesses and exercises the gift of infallibility in the Church, it is worth recalling the relationship which exists between *infallibility* and *truth*. Infallibility does not render a doctrine of the Church more true than it ever was. Infallibility is formally concerned not with the truth as such but rather with the *certitude* with which the truth is known. There are doctrines which are true but which have never been proclaimed infallibly; there are doctrines which have long been held to be true but are only proclaimed infallibly after a long passage of time in the Church's history; there are doctrines which are true, taught by the Church, but about which the Church does not have the absolute certitude which enables her to proclaim that truth definitively. There are degrees of certitude. Our very language reveals this. We say: "I think such and such is true," "Such and such seems to be true," "Such and such can't be wrong," "I am sure this is true," etc. Absolute certitude, on the other hand, expresses itself as "I know this is true" or "I am certain this is true." It is with this final certitude (a "definitive" decision as the Councils express it) that infallibility deals. The infallible doctrine of Mary's Immaculate Conception may serve as an example. The doctrine was being preached by some in the fifth century; it was preached and held by many in the thirteenth century (John Duns Scotus being an outstanding example); actively supported by the Popes from Sixtus IV in 1477; implicitly proclaimed by the Council of Trent in 1546 when it declared that its teaching on original sin was not meant to include Our Lady; forbidden to be spoken against by the theologians and faithful in 1617 and 1622; finally defined as a dogma of faith by Pius IX in 1854. Now the fact of Mary's immunity from all stain of original sin has been true since the time she was actually conceived in the womb of her mother. It is a truth, however, of which the Church became only gradually aware. This awareness was at first tentative, then seen as probable, and, gradually, with ever increasing certitude. The infallible proclamation of the fact of the Immaculate Conception thus added nothing to the factual truth of the dogma; it expressed rather the degree of certitude which the Church has of this fact.

As already seen, the entire Church will often hold a truth with certitude, i.e., infallibly, even though no Council or

Pope has proclaimed it as an infallible truth. Such is the nature of the infallibility of the whole People of God. At other times the Pope and bishops will be teaching a truth infallibly without proclaiming or defining it by a definitive *act* of Pope or council. In such a case we have the infallible exercise of the Ordinary Magisterium. And, at times, the Pope or a council will issue a definitive proclamation, thereby eliciting an infallible definition of the Extraordinary Magisterium.

The following schema may be of help in summarizing the preceding remarks on the *subject* of infallibility.

	Infallible	*Non-infallible*
Ordinary Magisterium (Pope and bishops teaching while dispersed throughout the world)	When they are teaching in harmony a truth which they say *must* be held definitively by all the faithful.	Any other instance of teaching on faith or morals.
Extraordinary Magisterium (Pope and bishops teaching while assembled in Council, or the Pope *defining* or *proclaiming* a doctrine definitively)	When a Council *defines* or definitively *proclaims* a truth, or when the Pope as head of the College of Bishops *defines* or *proclaims* a truth of faith or morals.	Any other instance of teaching on faith or morals.

The column marked "non-infallible" actually encompasses those teachings normally called *authoritative*. These are truths taught by the Church (through the Pope or the Pope and bishops or by an ecumenical council, etc.) for which less than a definitive degree of certitude is claimed. As already noted, the fact that such truths are not taught infallibly does not mean necessarily that they are not true, but rather that they lack the degree of certitude which enables the Church to teach something infallibly. Such truths as these will run a spectrum, each having its own degree of certitude. Some will be merely prudential decisions about what to believe or how to act; others will be probable; others relatively certain and intimately connected with truths already infallibly taught, etc. The degree of certitude which the Church attaches to such teaching can generally be gauged by how often the Church repeats the teaching, by the authority which proposes the teaching (e.g., whether the Pope, or a council, a congregation of the Roman Curia, a national episcopal conference, a resident bishop, etc.), by the nature of the matter involved, and other such considerations. Speaking of such authoritative teaching, the Second Vatican Council said:

> Bishops, teaching in communion with the Roman Pontiff, are to be respected by all as witnesses to divine and Catholic truth; moreover the faithful are to accept the teaching of their bishop concerning faith and morals as being offered in the name of Christ, and are to adhere to it with a religious submission of soul *(religioso animi obsequio adhaerere debent)*. Indeed, this religious submission of the will and the intellect is to be offered in a special way to the authentic magisterium of the Roman Pontiff even when he is not speaking *ex cathedra;* offered, that is, in such a way that his supreme magisterium is reverently acknowledged, the teaching proposed by him sincerely adhered to according to his clear intention and will which reveals itself especially from the nature of the documents [he issues], or from the frequency with which he proposes the same teaching, or from his manner of speaking *(Lumen Gentium,* no. 25).

Since, by the nature of the case, the certitude attached to the authoritative teachings of the Pope and bishops is less than definitive, i.e., is not infallible, it is clear that the "religious submission of mind and will" which the Church calls for from the faithful in such cases entails both docility and deep faith: docility to counteract the tendency to prefer our own ways of looking at matters and doing them; and faith which helps us realize that the authorities in the Church, even in proposing teaching which is less than definitively certain, are guided by the Holy Spirit in a way concomitant with the special responsibilities they have received.

History reveals that the Pope and bishops have not always been correct in all the matters which they have proposed as part of their authoritative teaching. Circumstances change, the matter is seen in a different perspective, new discoveries give greater insight, a more adequate grasp of the truth is had with the passage of time and, of course, the matter was never proposed by the Church with absolute certitude to begin with. Such being the case, it is not infrequently asked, "What is a Catholic to do if he or she cannot agree with an authoritative teaching of the Church?" Clearly the situation is different from that in which one is dealing with an infallible teaching of the Church, whether of her Ordinary or Extraordinary Magisterium. In this latter case, God has guaranteed the certitude of the truth in question and our consciences are faced with either assenting to His truth or rejecting His truth as it is offered to us with grace. The case of giving or withholding assent of mind and will to an authoritative teaching is not so clear. Indeed, the Church is aware that, in some cases, individuals or groups may find themselves in disagreement with one or another of her authoritative teachings. Such a position she respects if it is taken after much prayer, study, and a willingness to reexamine at opportune times the motives upon which a person bases his or her lack of agreement. The Church even recognizes the role of the various charisms or graces given by the Holy Spirit as well as the obligations which all the faithful have toward each other and toward those in authority in the Church, one of which obligations is the duty of fraternal correction.[7] Thus there is envisioned the possibility not only of withholding religious submission of mind and will to an authoritative teaching, but also of proposing one's own views for consideration by those in authority. Such a proposing of one's own views will take various forms depending on times and circumstances. However, the duties of "fraternal correction" should never be undertaken lightly; much less so in the case where one attempts (quite possibly misguidedly) to "correct" those God has placed over the Church. Great prudence, deep love for the Church and respect for those who guide her, as well as an active solicitude which seeks to avoid weakening the faith of others or of leading them into one's own possible error—all these are minimal virtues required of the person who would undertake such a task. Quite obviously, such virtues are antithetical to that type of activity which can only be labeled "organized dissent" to the teachings of the Church. Such dissent, grounded ultimately in arrogance and pride, can find no proper place in the Church which is not a political debating society but rather the Spouse of Christ and mediator of His truth and salvation. Moreover, if, after one's own views have been properly represented, the authorities continue to teach the same matter, a respectful silence is to be expected of those who still find themselves in a position of disagreement.

In the area of moral doctrine the matter of one's inability to agree with the Church's authoritative or authentic teaching offers special difficulties since, in this area, one is often dealing with issues which call for an immediate resolution. Something must either be acted upon or not. Treating of this specific topic the doctrinal committee of the Bishops of the United States recently wrote:

> In the area of moral doctrine, some have called attention to a theoretical possibility of error in some Church teaching.... But even when a teaching may not be infallibly proposed, it enjoys moral certitude, and, consequently, has a normative role in the formation of Christian conscience.[8]

If it is true to say that history gives evidence of cases where one or another authoritative teaching has in time proved to be an inadequate presentation of the truth or even actually wrong, it is also true to say that history demonstrates the relatively rare nature of such occurrences. Even in those cases where the Church has taught with a less than infallible certitude, history demonstrates that what she taught as the more probable course or the safer course or the more likely truth has, with the passage of time, proven to be, in the vast majority of such cases, a truth which ultimately was recognized as being certain.

It should be noted, finally, that it happens at times that teaching which seems to be proposed by the Church as authoritative is, in fact, a teaching being proposed as definitive by the Ordinary Magisterium or by the Pope. Such definitive teaching, as seen above and in Bishop Gasser's commentary, is infallible, incapable of being erroneous. The fact that such teaching may be proposed definitively but is done without a "definition" or "proclamation" with juridic or semi-juridic formulation by a council or Pope sometimes makes its character as infallible difficult to determine, as we have noted above when speaking of the infallible nature of the Ordinary Magisterium. The fact that such can and does happen, however, serves to indicate what careful study is needed in each case. Two extremes are to be avoided: 1) the tendency to what has been called "creeping infallibility" wherein everything taught by the Church is considered to have infallible certitude, and 2) the tendency to accept as true only what has been "defined" or "proclaimed" infallibly. Ultimately a trusting faith is called for. While the type of assent of mind and will which we give to the teaching of the Church will vary according to the degree of certitude with which the Church proposes the matter, it is to be recognized with confidence that God, who has instituted the Church for our salvation, will always preserve her authorities from teaching anything, over any long period of time, which could be detrimental to that salvation. It is such a realization which is the underpinning for the "religious submission of mind and will" which we give even to matters not infallibly taught.

II. The object of infallibility

As has already been noted, by the term *object* of infallibility theology proposes to answer the question, "What aspects of the truth are covered by the gift of infallibility—every truth, or only what God has directly revealed?"

It is clear from the very definition of *Pastor Aeternus* (cf. pp. 13-15 above) that the charism of infallibility has been given to the Church so that she be able to teach with certitude "doctrine of faith and morals." Long ago, however, Saint Thomas Aquinas noted that different truths pertain to the doctrine of faith and morals in various ways. Writing of heresy, he said:

> It must be said that by heresy we mean that which denotes a corruption of the Christian faith. Now if someone has a false opinion concerning those things which don't belong to the faith (e.g., matters of geometry or other such like), things which in no way can pertain to the faith, we are not speaking of the corruption of the faith in such cases. Rather we speak of the corruption of the faith only when someone has a false opinion concerning those things which pertain to the faith. Now something pertains to the faith in two ways: in one way, directly and principally, as, for example, the articles of the faith; the other way, indirectly and secondarily, as, for example, those things from which the corruption of some article of the faith would follow. Heresy, just like faith, can exist in respect to what pertains directly or indirectly *(S. Th., II, IIae, q. 11, a. 2 c)*.

Thus, Aquinas spoke of truths pertaining *directly* or *indirectly* to the faith. And theologians in general have followed his distinction, while adding, at times, any number of distinctions of their own. That which belongs *directly* to the faith is what the Church, following St. Paul in his letters to Timothy (cf. 1 Tim. 6:20 and 2 Tim. 1:14, the *ten [kalen] paratheken* in Greek), calls the *deposit of faith*. This deposit consists of the truths and way of life revealed to us by God—above all in the life and preaching of Jesus Christ—as that deposit is found, explicitly or implicitly, in Tradition and Sacred Scripture. That the Church is able to teach infallibly all the truths belonging to the deposit of faith is something recognized by all Catholics. Indeed, it is a matter of faith, taught—at least implicitly—by the First Vatican Council. As Bishop Gasser put it: "Hence it clearly is believed and must be believed as a matter of faith by all the children of holy Mother Church that the Church is infallible in proposing and defining dogmas of faith (cf. p. 76 above).

Aquinas noted, in the second place, that there are truths which belong *indirectly* to the faith. Following his lead and summarizing the teaching of the Church, Bishop Gasser said: "These truths, although they are not revealed *in se,* are nevertheless required in order to guard fully, explain properly and define efficaciously the very deposit of faith" (p. 76 above). Among such truths Gasser at Vatican I explicitly cited such things as "dogmatic facts" (cf. explanation on p. 79 above) and Joseph Kleutgen, at the same Council, mentioned the application of moral norms to new situations (cf. p. 82 above). Can the Church teach truths such as these infallibly? Aquinas had already noted that faith and heresy can exist in regard to such truths. Bishop Gasser stated at Vatican I that it was certain that such truths can be defined or proclaimed infallibly (cf. pp. 76-79 above), and it was the intention of the First Vatican Council to define that the Church could teach such truths infallibly (cf. pp. 82-83 above). Since it did not finish its work, that definition of faith was never made. Nevertheless, what Aquinas and Gasser held and what Vatican I intended to define, viz., that the Church can teach infallibly that which indirectly belongs to the deposit of faith, is taught by the Second Vatican Council and by post-conciliar documents (cf. pp. 82-83 above for discussion and texts).

Some theological dispute has arisen in our own day concerning this issue, although the dispute is generally limited to the realm of moral theology. Certain writers are of the opinion that the Church, while she is capable of giving authoritative teaching about *specific* rules to be followed in the conduct of a Christian life, cannot infallibly teach such specific rules. We may take as an example the Church's teaching on a relatively new moral problem, the artificial insemination of a woman who wants to bear a child and in which the implanted sperm comes from a donor who is not her husband. The Church has condemned the practice, i.e., she has authoritatively taught that such a procedure may not be morally done because it is contrary to the Creator's plan for human conception and offends the unitive purpose of the sexual act. The Church has not taught this infallibly and it is a matter clearly not found directly in the deposit of faith as that deposit shows itself in Scripture and Tradition. The question is: can the Church teach such a matter infallibly? The answer is certainly "yes," once it can be ascertained that such new and specific moral judgments pertain to those truths which, belonging to the indirect or secondary object of infallibility, are necessary to "guard fully, explain properly and define efficaciously the very deposit of faith." That such secondary objects of infallibility include new and specific moral norms was clearly the understanding of the bishops at Vatican I (cf. citation from the *relatio* of J. Kleutgen, pp. 69; 82-83 above) and has been, as Kleutgen points out in the same citation, the practice of the Church. Thus, although she has never defined this, the Church teaches that she has the authority from Christ to define infallibly such matters. Gasser remarked, "...whoever would deny that the Church or, equally, the Pope would be infallible in issuing such a decree would not as such be openly a heretic, but nevertheless would commit a most grave error and a very grave sin by erring in this way" (p. 81 above).[9]

In speaking of matters of moral conduct which pertain to the secondary or indirect *object* of infallibility, however, it is important to note that some matters which, at first glance, do not appear to be a part of the deposit of faith directly may, in fact, be so, and thereby pertain to the primary or direct object of infallibility. We may cite as an example the moral norm which declares that "every action which, either in anticipation of the conjugal act, or in its accomplishment, or in the development of its natural consequences, proposes, whether as an end or as a means, to render procreation impossible" (Encyclical *Humanae Vitae,* no. 14). This is the way Pope Paul VI phrased the Church's constant teaching on artificial contraception. It would seem, viewed superficially, that this teaching would pertain to those things which belong to the secondary object of infallibility; it would seem, that is, that such a teaching is not directly revealed, thus not forming part of the deposit of faith. Closer study indicates, however, that such is not the case. Pope John Paul II has written:

> The author of the encyclical stresses that this norm belongs to the "natural law," that is to say, it is in accordance with reason as such. The Church teaches this norm, although it is not formally (that is, literally) expressed in Sacred Scripture, and it does this in the conviction that the interpretation of the precepts of natural law belongs to the competence of the Magisterium.
>
> However, we can say more. Even if the moral law, formulated in this way in the Encyclical *Humanae Vitae,* is not found literally in Sacred Scripture, nonetheless, from the fact that it is contained in Tradition and—as Pope Paul VI writes—has been "very often expounded by the Magisterium" (HV 12) to the faithful, it follows that this norm is in accordance with the sum total of revealed doctrine contained in biblical sources (HV 4).
>
> It is a question here not only of the sum total of the moral doctrine contained in Sacred Scripture, of its essential premises and the general character of its content, but of that fuller context to which we have previously dedicated numerous analyses when speaking about the "theology of the body."
>
> Precisely against the background of this full context it becomes evident that the above mentioned moral norm belongs not only to the natural moral law, but also to the *moral order revealed by God* (Pope John Paul II, *Reflections on Humanae Vitae,* St. Paul Editions, Boston, 1984, pp. 9-10).

What the Holy Father is saying is that this moral norm, although not found explicitly or "literally" in Sacred Scripture, forms, nonetheless, part of the revealed moral order and is found *implicitly* in the sources of Revelation, Sacred Scripture and Tradition. Therefore it belongs to the deposit of faith as well as to the natural moral law, and so is included among the truths which fall under the primary object of infallibility. This fact indicates how difficult it is at times to determine, *a priori*, whether something is *implicitly* revealed or whether it belongs to those secondary truths which are necessary to "guard fully, explain properly and define efficaciously the very deposit of faith." Even the case cited above (i.e., the case of artificial insemination of a woman with sperm not that of her husband) as belonging to the truths contained in the "secondary" object of infallibility may, in fact, be a truth implicitly revealed and, as such, belong to the primary object of infallibility. Often only history and the Church's developing awareness of the truths committed to her—an awareness guided by the Holy Spirit—provide the means to make such a determination.

In respect to the object of infallibility—whether it be primary or secondary—it should be noted finally that what belongs to the *object* of infallibility need never be taught infallibly. When one treats of the object of infallibility one is discussing those truths *capable* of being taught infallibly, either by the Ordinary or Extraordinary Magisterium. For various reasons, however, some truths capable of being taught infallibly by the Church's Magisterium are not, in fact, taught definitively. Generally this happens when such truths are unquestioned, no opportunity thereby providing for or necessitating a definitive teaching.

In the introduction to his Gospel St. Luke stated to Theophilus that he was writing it so that one might have certainty about the things which have been taught (cf. Lk. 1:4). In the Church it is the Holy Spirit Himself and the gift of infallibility which He bestows on the Church which maintains us in that certitude. This gift, however, does not mean that all the truths proclaimed by the Church infallibly are of equal importance. Indeed, the *Decree on Ecumenism* of Vatican Council II reminded us of this fact when it said:

> In comparing doctrines they (i.e., Catholic theologians) should remember that there exists an order or "hierarchy" of the truths of Catholic doctrine since these truths have a diverse connection with the foundation of Christian faith *(Unitatis Redintegratio,* no. 11).

The truth which that statement enunciates should be obvious. The mysteries of the Trinity, the Incarnation of the eternal Son by the Holy Spirit of the Virgin Mary, the Eucharist, the Church and other such doctrines are more central to the mystery of God Himself than such doctrines as the existence of angels or even infallibility. Nonetheless, whatever their place in the "hierarchy of truths" all the doctrines are true, each having its own relative place of importance in the knowledge we have of God Himself and the visible and invisible universe He has created and redeemed. Flowing from God Himself, the fountain of all truth, all the doctrines, whatever their order in the hierarchy of truth, are intimately related and history has shown that a denial of even "minor" ones generally involves a subsequent weakening of one's faith in those which are more central. What St. Paul wrote of the different members of the Body of Christ has relevance here.

> ...those members of the body that appear to be weaker are necessary, and the members we consider less honorable we treat with special honor (1 Cor. 12:22).

So it is with the doctrines of the Faith. God has seen fit to let us know them with certitude and so we accept them all and guard them, realizing that we never understand the full importance of any of them and that each of them is but one more insight into His goodness and wisdom. Speaking of this "hierarchy of truth," the Church has said further:

> It is true that there exists an order and as it were a hierarchy of the Church's dogmas, as a result of their varying relationship to the foundation of the faith. This hierarchy means that some dogmas are founded

on other dogmas which are the principal ones, and are illuminated by these latter. But all dogmas, since they are revealed, must be believed with the same divine faith.[10]

Not only do the truths have a varied relationship to one another, they also have a varied relationship to the history of the Church and to the different ages and cultures in which she has lived and lives. This fact can lead to the realization that some truths will be more important at a particular time than others, that the significance of the truths will vary as they are seen at different times and in a wider framework as the Church's awareness of the mystery entrusted to her develops and even that, at times, the way the truths have been expressed can bear traces of a "worldview" or language which has subsequently greatly changed. Such realizations, however, should never lead to the conclusion that the truths are only relative in the sense that they are suitable for only a particular period or place.

> The faithful must shun the opinion, first, that dog-matic formulas (or some category of them) cannot sig-nify truth in a determinate way, but can only offer changeable approximations to it, which to a certain extent distort or alter it; secondly, that these formulas signify the truth only in an indeterminate way, this truth being like a goal that is constantly being sought by means of such approximations. Those who hold such an opinion do not avoid dogmatic relativism and they corrupt the concept of the Church's infallibility relative to the truth to be taught or held in a determi-nate way.[11]

The Church indeed is able to express the truth in various ways and she is capable of taking a previously taught truth and offering it to us in a new *formulation* which may be bet-ter suited to new times and circumstances. She can do so, however, only by retaining all of the "meaning" of the truth contained in the earlier formulation since the *"meaning* of dogmatic formulas remains ever true and constant in the Church even when it is expressed with greater clarity or more developed."[12]

We may use as an example of this the case of the man who enters a room paved with an intricate and beautiful mosaic floor. He may at first notice the brightly colored blue fish at one end of the mosaic. He remarks upon it, stating that it is both blue and beautiful. He then proceeds to take in to his vision other aspects of the mosaic, commenting on each in turn. Finally he steps back to get an overall view of the entire piece, noticing while he does so that each individual piece, while being all that he saw and commented on originally takes on a different perspective when seen in conjunction with the entire masterpiece. So it happens, in a way, when the Church expresses the truths committed to her. Each of the individual truths which she infallibly teaches remains true as originally seen, but the perspective can change as more and more of the truth is seen, and this greater perspective enables her to express the truth with greater clarity and in a more developed manner without in any way losing the insight and truth first glimpsed. Even the Church, of course, will never get the full perspective until we all see God Himself face to face. In that vision every truth the Church has ever taught infallibly will be seen in its full significance, having lost nothing of its own meaning but rather having taken on new depths of intelligibility and beauty when faith gives place to sight.

Complex as some of the issues are when treating of the gift of infallibility which God has given to His Church, the essence of the doctrine is essentially simple. On the night in which He instituted the Eucharist, Jesus promised His disciples that He would send them the Holy Spirit. He Himself described this Spirit as the "Spirit of truth" who "will lead you into all truth" (Jn. 16:13). The gift of infallibility is but the extension of that greater Gift by which we are led into truth and preserved from error.

Footnotes

1. J.H. Newman, *An Essay On the Development of Christian Doctrine,* Image Books, Doubleday and Co., Garden City, N.Y., 1960, pp. 105-107.

2. *Letter of John Paul II to German Bishops,* May 15, 1980, *The Pope Speaks,* vol. 25, no. 3, p. 243.

3. Henri de Lubac, S.J., *The Splendour of the Church,* Deus Books, Paulist Press, Glen Rock, N.J., 1963, pp. 166-169.

4. J. H. Newman, *On Consulting the Faithful in Matters of Doctrine,* 1871 version, edited and introduced by John Coulson, Sheed and Ward, N.Y., 1961, p. 63.

5. The "only" in this statement was objected to by Karl Rahner when the Congregation for the Doctrine of the Faith repeated the statement in the declaration *Mysterium Ecclesiae.* His reservations were aimed at preserving a place in the Church for the exercise of non-hierarchical contributions to the Church's teaching mission (cf. "Mysterium Ecclesiae," *Theological Investigations,* vol. XVII, p. 144). That this desideratum can be achieved without the removal of the "only" in the Conciliar statement is an evident fact. Many groups and individuals, not least of them being parents, exercise a form of "magisterium" in the Church which is, in fact, indispensable. The value and necessity of such exercises of the prophetic mission of the whole people of God—as well as avoiding among them a constant quarreling to determine which is the more essential—is, in fact, safeguarded by the recognition among such groupings that there is ultimately *one* Magisterium which authoritatively speaks for Christ.

6. Pius XII, "Address 'Si diligis' of May 31, 1954," *TPS,* second quarter, 1954, p. 154.

7. On fraternal correction of superiors in the Church, cf. St. Thomas, *S. Th.,* II, IIae, q. 33, a. 4. Indeed all of question 33 is pertinent and it should be noted that it all falls under his general treatment of charity.

8. Committee on Doctrine of the National Conference of Catholic Bishops, *Statement on Fr. Richard McBrien's "Catholicism,"* July 5, 1985, p. 5.

9. On the Church's ability to define specific moral norms, cf. Germain Grisez, "Infallibility and Specific Moral Norms: A Review Discussion," *The Thomist,* 49, 2, pp. 248ff. In defending the position that the Church can teach infallibly specific moral norms, Grisez disputes the position of Rev. Francis Sullivan, S.J. as expressed in Sullivan's work *Magisterium: Teaching Authority in the Catholic Church* (Paulist Press, N.Y., 1983). Part of the dispute revolves around their different interpretations of Gasser's *relatio.* It would appear to me that Grisez's understanding of Gasser is clearly the correct one.

10. "Mysterium Ecclesiae," trans. by Austin Flannery, O.P., *Vatican Council II,* vol. II, Costello Pub. Co., Northport, New York, 1982, p. 433.

11. *Idem,* p. 434.

12. *Ibid.*

The FATHER'S SON

Rev. James T. O'Connor

ORDER FROM:

DAUGHTERS OF ST. PAUL
50 ST. PAUL'S AVE.
JAMAICA PLAIN
BOSTON, MA 02130

ACCOUNT NUMBER_____

NAME _____

ORGANIZATION_____

    OR PARISH_____

STREET_____

CITY_____STATE_____ZIP _____

_____PAYMENT ENCLOSED   _____PLEASE BILL ME

20% discount to clergy and religious

Prepaid orders: 75¢ postage for one book and 20¢ for each additional one.

Daughters of St. Paul

MASSACHUSETTS
50 St. Paul's Ave., Jamaica Plain, Boston, MA 02130 **617-522-8911.**
172 Tremont Street, Boston, MA 02111 **617-426-5464; 617-426-4230.**

NEW YORK
78 Fort Place, Staten Island, NY 10301 **718-447-5071; 718-447-5086.**
59 East 43rd Street, New York, NY 10017 **212-986-7580.**
625 East 187th Street, Bronx, NY 10458 **212-584-0440.**
525 Main Street, Buffalo, NY 14203 **716-847-6044.**

NEW JERSEY
Hudson Mall Route 440 and Communipaw Ave.,
Jersey City, NJ 07304 **201-433-7740.**

CONNECTICUT
202 Fairfield Ave., Bridgeport, CT 06604 **203-335-9913.**

OHIO
2105 Ontario Street (at Prospect Ave.), Cleveland, OH 44115 **216-621-9427.**
616 Walnut Street, Cincinnati, OH 45202 **513-421-5733; 513-721-5059.**

PENNSYLVANIA
1719 Chestnut Street, Philadelphia, PA 19103 **215-568-2638; 215-864-0991.**

VIRGINIA
1025 King Street, Alexandria, VA 22314 **703-549-3806.**

SOUTH CAROLINA
243 King Street, Charleston, SC 29401 **803-577-0175.**

FLORIDA
2700 Biscayne Blvd., Miami, FL 33137 **305-573-1618.**

LOUISIANA
4403 Veterans Memorial Blvd. Metairie, LA 70006 **504-887-7631; 504-887-0113.**
423 Main Street, Baton Rouge, LA 70802 **504-343-4057; 504-381-9485.**

MISSOURI
1001 Pine Street (at North 10th), St. Louis, MO 63101 **314-621-0346.**

ILLINOIS
172 North Michigan Ave., Chicago, IL 60601 **312-346-4228; 312-346-3240.**

TEXAS
114 Main Plaza, San Antonio, TX 78205 **512-224-8101.**

CALIFORNIA
1570 Fifth Ave. (at Cedar Street), San Diego, CA 92101 **619-232-1442.**
46 Geary Street, San Francisco, CA 94108 **415-781-5180.**

WASHINGTON
2301 Second Ave., Seattle, WA 98121 **206-441-3300.**

HAWAII
1143 Bishop Street, Honolulu, HI 96813 **808-521-2731.**

ALASKA
750 West 5th Ave., Anchorage, AK 99501 **907-272-8183.**

CANADA
3022 Dufferin Street, Toronto 395, Ontario, Canada.